Songs In The Night

SONGS in the NIGHT

Holding on in the darkness of life.

D. B. (DEE) SHELNUTT, JR.

XULON PRESS

Xulon Press
2301 Lucien Way #415
Maitland, FL 32751
407.339.4217
www.xulonpress.com

© 2019 by D. B. (Dee) Shelnutt, Jr.

All rights reserved solely by the author. The author guarantees all contents are original and do not infringe upon the legal rights of any other person or work. No part of this book may be reproduced in any form without the permission of the author. The views expressed in this book are not necessarily those of the publisher.

Unless otherwise indicated, all Biblical references are from The New Revised Standard Version. Copyright © 1991 by Oxford University Press, Inc. Division of Christian Education of National Council of the Churches of Christ In the United States of America.

Unless noted all hymn references are from The United Methodist Hymnal. Copyright © 1989 by the United Methodist Publishing House.

All Biblical references are taken from the New Revised Standard Version. Copyright © 1991 by the Division of Christian Education of the National Council of the Churches of Christ in the United States of America,

Abbreviations:

NRSV: The New Revised Standard Version
UMH: United Methodist Hymnal.

Printed in the United States of America.

ISBN-13: 9781545676530

Dedication

To: Almighty God who gives us songs in the night!

To: all who have helped me to know the words to God's songs in the darkness of my life

Table of Contents

Acknowledgements ix
Introduction. xiii
A True Story xix

Chapter 1	The Song of Presence	1
Chapter 2	The Song of Endurance	11
Chapter 3	The Song of Generosity.	21
Chapter 4	The Song of Community	35
Chapter 5	The Song of Example	49
Chapter 6	The Song of Laughter	57
Chapter 7	The Song of Forgiveness.	63
Chapter 8	The Song of the Child	73
Chapter 9	The Song of Hope	81
Chapter 10	The Song of Love	89
Chapter 11	The Song of Light	97
Chapter 12	The Song of Joy.	105
Chapter 13	The Song of Songs.	113

Acknowledgements

No man is an island entire of itself; every man
is a piece of the continent, a part of the main;
if a clod be washed away by the sea, Europe
is the less, as well as if a promontory were, as
well as any manner of thy friends or of thine
own were; any man's death diminishes me,
because I am involved in mankind.
And therefore, never send to know for whom
the bell tolls; it tolls for thee.
John Donne*

John Donne had it right in his famed poem, "No man is an island." The writing of a book of any kind is never the work of the author alone. Truth be known, almost every person in one's life has an impact on each page written. To try to name them all would be futile. Instead, let me thank those who have helped me to make this particular resource possible:

- All the people mentioned in this work who have left indelible impressions upon my soul.
- My family: wife: Kandy – the wind beneath my wings, My children: Meredith (husband Jordan) their children Georgia, Elizabeth and Anna; Emory (wife Amanda) and his son Parker and step-son, Max; Wesley (wife Melissa)

Songs In The Night

- Davis Chappell – brotha – enough said!
- Jeff and Ruth Watkins, Kim and Nancy Treaster, Mike and Kathy Potts; dearest friends
- Andrew Adams Webb – kindred spirit
- Don Overton – my bbq buddy! You and Heidi are wonderful!
- Christy Hinson – PHS
- Doug and Sandra Barge, Chris and Amy and their family
- Martha Strickland – a strength to my soul
- Carolyn Barnett, Willie and Sue Wilson, Allan and Lura Landis, Margaret Littlefield, the sistren Dennis, Jim and Marie Sams, Fletcher and Dana Sams, Ferrol and Kathy Sams– Jeff and Patti Ellis, Chris and Susan Parrott, Phyllis Williamson and Diane Weis for being who you are!
- Britt and Angie Matthiessen, - forever friends
- Jim McNeely, my proofreader, friend and fellow UGA fan. Throughout the years, he has edited my work and given fresh insights and wisdom. You will always be my "booger hollow" bud!
- Tom Fishburne – friend, advisor, supporter (and in memory of Dana)
- Betty Jennings, Betty Hampton, Rich and Elizabeth Harris – lifetime friends
- Charles and Myrlene Barnes – my "second" parents!
- Crazy 8's: Mike/Chris Selleck, Terry/Sharon Walton, Steve/Bunny Winter
- Jim (and Sharon) Renken, friend who continually prompts me to write
- Dr. E. Marston Rascoe, friend, confidant, encourager, mentor, advisor

---

*Donne, John. Devotions Upon Emergent Occasions, Meditation 17, "No Man is an Island. 1624

Acknowledgements

- Sharman Pirkle – inspiration and dear friend
- Greg Casto – my cohort in finding the best cheeseburgers in the world!
- Steve Brooks – my beloved walking buddy!
- Bo and Sally Walpole, Chuck Hodges, Grady Mosley, Jeff Lewandowski, Julie Boone, Jerry Ward, Steve Huffstetler, Gary Billings, Luke Haymond, Mathew Pinson, Phil Smelley, Rick and Jeannine Massengale, Bob and Robin Bowling, Ron Capes, Paul Freeman, Kirby Pate, Kep Pate. Frank and Terri Parker, Steve Peek, Jeff Burnette, Jack Mayo, Brian Tillman, Brian Funderburke, Brian Overstreet, Bryan and Debbie Benfield, Clint and Jane Emerson, Craig and Cheryl Collins, Brian and Laurie Mcgee, Calvin Haney, Lisa Carlisle, Ed and Sheree Whigham, Ashley Lebovitz, Michael and Stephanie Young, Dave and Lonna Upton, Chris and Brook Jefts, Randy and Diane Roberts, Tim and Julie Milam, Bob and Sharon Reno, Tom and Paige Webster, David Elrod, Brad Elrod, Bob Hope, Ron Greer and Sister Sanko and the Dixie Pigs!
- Eva Carrazales, Nell and Liz Burch, and Laura Jane Nestlehutt
- The late: Arnold Gardner, Frank Orr, Christopher Carlton, Bobbie Hayes, Virginia Harlow, Bill Ziegler, Sarah Lee Abercrombie, Bob Brooks, Lucille Taylor, Robert Preston Price, Lucille Collins, Velma Roberts, David Fox, Annetta Graydon, Wilton Moulder, Bill and Carolyn Self, Vince Norton, Mickey Littlefield, Susan Hope, Eula Braswell, Doug Strickland and my parents: Dumas and Tex Shelnutt
- Cousins: Judy Riddell, Joy Privett, Jolli Weaver, George Dyson and their families.
- My siblings, Jan, Debbie and Mark
- The people of the churches I have been honored to serve over forty years in ministry:

Owl Rock United Methodist Church
Atlanta, Georgia
Fayetteville First United Methodist Church
Fayetteville, Georgia
McKendree United Methodist Church
Lawrenceville, Georgia
Rock Springs United Methodist Church
Buford, Georgia
North Fayette United Methodist Church
Fayetteville, Georgia
Saint Timothy United Methodist Church
Stone Mountain, Georgia
Augusta District/Cabinet of the North Georgia Conference of the
United Methodist Church
Augusta, Georgia
Johns Creek United Methodist Church
Johns Creek, Georgia

INTRODUCTION
Darkness Comes

The darkness from the natural pattern of night and day calls us to lie down and sleep making us feel refreshed when we awaken. This darkness can allow us to see the beauty of stars and the moon. It can accent the surroundings of a campfire in the midst of the woods as we sit around and tell stories, heat a marshmallow, or simply lie back and peer into the flames, which emit both an indescribable glow and a sense of peace.

Darkness comes in other ways. Sometimes it comes to us creeping in on our lives like a violent storm, even like a hurricane blowing everything around us into a world we no longer recognize. All people have experienced this darkness in some way. It comes to us in the death of a loved one, the death of a marriage, a job, a friendship, a dream, our health, our world as we know it and in multitudes of other ways. What do we do with when it comes our way? How can we hold on when the darkness of life seems to consume us, paralyze us, shake our foundations, and even our faith in ourselves and those we have loved and cherish?

How many times have we lain in the bed in the middle of the night, stunned and saddened and no words come to mind for us to even describe the pain and fear? We think of God but wonder if

God is there. We may think of praying but no words surface, and we are left to feel abandoned and alone. The darkness covers us almost to the point of suffocation. What do we do? Where do we go? To whom do we listen? What is 'out-there' that can bring us hope when hopelessness seems to envelope us?

Almost from the start of my life, death and pain have been constant companions. In kindergarten, one of my classmates died of leukemia. In elementary school I had two friends who were killed in automobile accidents as well as the tragic death of a close friend's father. In middle school, a friend went to a party and tried alcohol for the first time. In his drunkenness, he found a car with keys in it and drove it down the driveway into the streets, driving wildly until he had a head-on collision killing himself and the man in the other car: my Sunday school teacher!

High school was difficult in that it was the first year of racial integration. The first football game of the "new" combined schools was tense. My father was a pastor and a member of his church brought a shotgun to the stadium and killed a black student. The small town where we lived was in turmoil. Going to school each day was a harrowing experience. There were knifings, threats, and fights. In addition to all of this, one of my closest high school friends was killed and later another friend in a tragic car accident.

My sophomore year in college was one of great tragedy. Six friends died in six weeks. One drowned scuba diving in Florida, another asleep at the wheel of her car causing it to wreck and the car exploding into flames. She was identified only by her necklace and dental records. Yet, another friend was decapitated in a car accident, two others in separate automobile accidents where they were not driving, but passengers. Another died from a brain tumor.

The cumulative weight of these deaths was a lot for anyone, but particularly for a 19-year-old. They led me to go to a counselor. For nine months, I had intensive sessions on the meaning of life and the mystery of death. It was during these days of great soul-searching that I felt called forth into ministry. I knew I might never be a great pastor, preacher, administrator, or anything else, but I knew what it was like to feel the pain of loss. I knew the intense suffering one experiences when the call comes with the news that a tragedy has happened.

For over forty years I have been a pastor in the United Methodist ministry, serving as pastor to six churches, and being with beloved people in their sickness, suffering, dying and deaths. I am not an expert in counseling the bereaved, nor do I have the answers to all of life's pivotal questions. What I have learned is that God is always with us in the darkest times of life and there is no darkness so deep that the light of God's presence cannot penetrate it.

This book bears witness that "in the night, God's songs shall always be with us." God has a song for us all and my prayer is that we will hear it and find peace.

D. B. (Dee) Shelnutt, Jr.
Sweet Harbor
Gainesville, Georgia
Summer, 2019

In the night God's song shall be with me*

*Psalm 42:8b

What tho' my joys and comforts die?
The Lord my Savior liveth;
What tho' the darkness gather round?
Songs in the night he giveth.

No storm can shake my inmost calm
While to that refuge clinging;
Since Christ is Lord of heaven and earth,
How can I keep from singing?*

Lowery, Robert Wadsworth. Bright Jewels for the Sunday School. 1869

A True Story

There is a tribe in Africa where the birth date of a child is counted – not from when they're born, nor from when they are conceived—but from the day that the child was a thought in its mother's mind.

And when a woman decides that she will have a child, she goes off and sits under a tree, by herself, and she listens until she can hear the song of the child that wants to come. And after she's heard the song of this child, she comes back to the man who will be the child's father, and she teaches it to him. And then, when they make love to physically conceive the child, some of that time they sing the song of the child, as a way to invite it.

And then, when the mother is pregnant, the mother teaches that child's song to the midwives and the old women of the village, so that when the child is born, the old women and the people around her sing the child's song to welcome it. And then, as the child grows up, the other villagers are taught the child's song. If the child falls, or hurts its knee, someone picks it up and sings its song to it. Or perhaps the child does something wonderful or goes through the rites of puberty – then as a way of honoring this person, the people of the village sing his or her song.

And it goes on this way through their life – in marriage, the songs are sung, together. And finally, when this child is lying in

Songs In The Night

bed, ready to die, all the villagers know his or her song, and they sing--- for the last time- -the song to that person. *

God gives us all songs. From the beginning of recorded time we hear that God sings, and the world comes into being. God sings and there appears sun and moon and stars, mountains and lakes, fish in the seas and animals of the land. God sings and male and female are created. God sings, and history begins. God's songs continue to help us know who we are and whose we are. What are God's songs given to you? Here are some of mine:

*Muller, Wayne. How then Shall We Live. Penguin/Random Press, 1997, Page 6

CHAPTER 1

The Song of Presence

Upon arriving in Fayette County to begin my work as a youth minister on my summer break from seminary, I found myself on a staff of mostly older people with one exception: the Barge family. Sandra was the church's organist and she and her husband, Doug, were parents of Chris, Stacey and Amy. I soon would learn that Doug was one of a gazillion family members in the church and that Sandra was related to many in the county. They were a beloved family entrenched in both the church and community.

During my years there, I spent many Sunday afternoons eating at the Barge's table, weekends with them at various camping spots in the North Georgia mountains, and time together at extra-curricular church events. They loved so many of the things I enjoyed doing. They became "family" to me.

One Sunday evening, I was on my way from my office into the sanctuary for evening worship when nine-year-old Stacey ran around the corner and right into me. I picked him up, held him in my arms and said, "It would be best not to run in the church, you could get hurt." He hugged me, jumped down and rapidly walked back to wherever it was he had come.

When the service began that evening, I sat with him and his siblings on the pew next to the piano where his mother was playing. I watched him holding the hymnal and singing the great hymns of the faith. He was a bright and precious little boy.

Following that evening's worship, I spent the night at my parent's home, so I could do some study at Emory University the next day. They lived two blocks from campus making it easy for me to walk and not have to fight parking issues.

On that Monday, following my morning study at Emory, I returned to my folk's house for lunch just as the phone rang. It was the pastor of the church where I worked. He said there had been an accident. A crane on a Fulton County work truck had gotten caught in telephone wires and when the operator tried to untangle it, the crane fell. It fell into the van containing Sandra and the children. Stacey was the only one of the children in the back seat and he was sitting exactly where the crane landed killing him instantly.

I felt numb all over. It couldn't be! I had just held him in my arms the night before. I was at their home on Saturday eating pizza. Dead? It couldn't be! My father came in for lunch and when I told him what had happened, he said, "Let's go to Fayette County and see the family. What would I say? What could I say? My heart was in pieces.

When we arrived at the house, cars were parked everywhere. It seemed the whole county had gathered to grieve with the family. We were greeted at the door by the pastor of the church. He and my father and I walked down the hallway to Sandra's bedroom where she was lying on the bed. She raised up and hugged Dad and then me.

When she put her head back down on the pillow, she looked up at me and said, "I know I am going to get through this because Eleanor just came to see me."

Eleanor was a woman in the church and community who was the mother of four children. Her eldest son, at age four, died on the operating table from an allergic reaction to anesthesia during a simple tonsillectomy. Her grief was profound. She had many dark days but, she kept on going. She would tear up at things most people would never understand; she laughed and smiled in joy from what the world would simply pass by. But Eleanor was one who would not let death or grief defeat her

When she heard about the accident, Eleanor jumped in her car and went straight to Sandra's home. She did not have to say a word. She did not have do a thing. All she did was show up and it was enough. None of the clergy could do for Sandra and Doug what Eleanor did by her silent presence.

Many years later, friends of ours found their 25 year-old-son dead from suicide. After spending time with the family as their pastor, I slipped quietly into another room of the house and called Don. Five years earlier, Don had lost his 16 year-old-son to suicide. I told him what had happened and simply asked him to come to the house. He asked the same question I had asked my Dad when I learned about Stacey, "What can I say?" I told Don, "Don't prepare anything to say. Please, just come. Let them see you. Your very presence will give them hope and strength and courage that no one else can give."

I was watching for Don when I heard the doorbell ring. When Don entered the house the hug Don gave to Jeff and Ruth lifted their spirits in ways that were visibly seen. He had no answers. He had no words of wisdom to give, but his presence as one who had been there spoke loudly.

When my mother had to have a radical mastectomy in the mid 1970's, all of her children and relatives surrounded her with love and support. However, it was the visit of a perfect stranger that helped my mother toward greater healing than anyone. She came into Mom's room and closed the door. She told her that she had had the same surgery. She told mother what it was like to undress in front of her husband the first time. She related how it felt to have to buy a prosthesis, wear a wig and dress differently than before the surgery. She showed mother her scars. When she left the room, Mother was smiling for the first time and talked about going home.

In my own life I remember receiving the news that a dear friend had been killed when the horse he was riding accidently slipped on oily pavement and fell causing my friend to hit his head on the cement curb of the street. I was in shock, disbelief, and denial. Later that day, my father said, "Let's go to the funeral home to visit the family." I asked, "Will Bill be ready to be seen?" He said, "Yes. Let's go."

I dreaded getting there. We walked into the room where the family was supposed to be, but it was empty. Then I noticed the coffin. Slowly, I walked over to it and looked in. There was Bill. The tears began to pour down my face. I felt an acute emptiness until I felt the arm of my father coming around me and pulling me close to him. He did not say one word. We simply held onto each other as we looked for the last time upon one we had loved. It was enough. We went home, back to the routine of life. But I have never forgotten the feel and the ministry of my father's arms around me in my dark night of the soul. His presence was all that I needed, because there were no answers. There were no simple words to eliminate such great grief. He spoke volumes through his caring embrace. His presence with me was enough; indeed, more than enough. I walked out of that funeral home with more strength and peace than when I went in.

The ministry of presence is crucial.

When darkness comes upon us in our lives, who are the ones who have walked before us, have endured the same, and have come out on the other side victoriously? Call them. Remember them. Be in their presence.

The Song Of Presence

If you do not know anyone, look up churches in your area and see if they have support groups. During my years as pastor in my last pastorate, the church began nineteen such groups.

One year, the church experienced the loss of several children; some from disease, accidents or suicide. Since there were no support groups in the community to aid the parents, our church began a chapter of Compassionate Friends. Within a few weeks, the room was filled with grieving parents seeking the presence of others who "had been there."

Other support groups began to form: divorce care, widow's support, widowers support, bi-polar-depression, grief support, Rainbows (for children who have been experienced a traumatic death in their lives), PFLAG (parent and friends of lesbians and gays), Can-care (a one-on-one support from a person who has the same cancer), prostate support, cancer support, financial help support, job networking, Stephen Ministry, and suicide prevention, Alcoholics Anonymous, Al-anon, Narcotics Anonymous, and Nar-anon. The PFLAG groups have expanded to include persons and families who have a loved one trans-gendering (there are now three large rooms filled each month for this alone.) On Tuesday evenings, the church is filled with people who are, as the late Henri Nouwen called them, "wounded healers." * All of us are wounded in some way, and many are able to share their wounds and listen to others with similar wounds, in ways that are healing to others.

Interestingly, the Barges continue their work in the church helping with children's and music ministries, Jeff and Ruth, parents of the 25-year-old who took his life are now Stephen Ministers and Don, who lost his 16-year-old son to suicide, is a leader with Compassionate Friends. They are "wounded healers" and have brought great comfort and peace to those fresh in the grieving process.

*Nouwen, Henri. The Wounded Healer. Ministry in Contemporary Society. Image Publishers. 1979.

One of the reasons the cross is the pivotal point of human history is that Jesus' suffering and death is something that is translatable to all people. He knew the feeling of betrayal, he suffered the pain of rejection, he felt the brutality of physical abuse as he was nailed to the tree. He has been there. He knew darkness, profound grief and sorrow.

He is with us. And He will be with us until the end of the age. His very presence is empowering and strengthening. He is with us – and mostly we don't need words, we just need Him. Many people carry crosses in their pockets, purses, or around their necks to hold in times of loss and crisis. The cross reminds them and all of us of his eternal presence that can bring peace.

The steeples on the top of many churches are a reminder that God took a negative and turned it into a positive in the life of Jesus of Nazareth and what God did for Him, God can do for us. It is the symbol that death is a reality, yet it is not the final word. God has the final word. The final word is Easter, which means, salvation, peace, forgiveness, wholeness, redemption and new life. It means we are never alone. Never! Not in darkness, not in crisis, not in tragedy, not in death.

When I married, I had never been on an airplane or a cruise ship. I was scared to death to experience both. We flew 1600 miles over the ocean and as the captain of the plane announced that we should prepare to land, my stomach began to turn, anxiety mounting. We would land in a country far away from home. I looked out the plane's window and the first thing I saw, towering above the clouds, was the steeple on the top of a cathedral. Seeing it, my body and mind began to relax as I realized that God already was there before I arrived. God was there as God was in America. I was not alone. No matter what happened on my honeymoon as my new wife and I traveled to various countries, the assurance of God's never-ending presence and love would be with us. The words of Psalm 23 rang out like a symphony filling the skies with the words "fear not, for I am with you."

"In the night, God's song shall be with us." One of them is the song of presence.

No wonder birds sing in the morning the song given to them in the night.
(copied)

Chapter 2

The Song of Endurance

How many times have we tried something new and quit after one or two tries? How many times have we invested our time and efforts in people only for them to let us down? How often do we feel God has left us alone in this huge universe especially when a friend has betrayed us, the doctor says, "there is nothing we can do", the pink slip is handed to us, the love of our life says, "I want a divorce", or a child has gone into the "far" country of drugs and alienation?

A few years ago, one of my closest friends, took his life. (When I arrived at the emergency room, he was still alive but died a few hours later. I put the sign of the cross on his forehead as I prayed for him. I told him he was loved by all the people who knew him. I assured him that his young family would be taken care of by family, friends and the church. For four hours, we sat around him, talking to him, patting his arms and hands, expressing our love to him. And then the end came.) I, along with hundreds of others, were shocked, stunned, devastated, angry, sad, and overwhelmed.

His death was traumatic for me. I loved him like a brother. We were kindred spirits in numerous ways. He suffered from bi-polar disorder. Everyday was a struggle for him to keep his moods in balance. Most of the time he was easy to be around, humorous, smart and caring. Then there were days he would spiral downward into dark depression. He would constantly say to those he counseled "even if you feel like taking your life, don't ever do it." He meant it. He was an expert in pastoral care, but I soon learned that "even the experts can lose their way." In his "right" mind, he would never have hurt himself, and I know he would never want to cause those of us who loved him, to be left with great sorrow and pain.

His funeral was held in the church where I was the pastor. Almost two thousand people filled the sanctuary.

Before I rose to deliver a eulogy, the chancel choir of the church stood and sang "My Shepherd will supply all my needs". I listened carefully to the words from the Twenty-Third Psalm:

My Shepherd will supply my need; Jehovah is His Name;
In pastures fresh He makes me feed beside the living stream.
He brings my wand'ring spirit back when I forsake His ways,
And leads me, for His mercy's sake, in paths of truth and grace.
When I walk thru the shades of death, Thy presence is my stay;
A word of Thy supporting breath drives all my fears away.
Thy hand, in sight of all my foes, doth still my table spread;
My cup with blessings overflows; thine oil anoints my head.
The sure provisions of my God attend me all my days;
O may Thy house be mine abode, and all my work be praise!
There would I find **a settled rest** (while others go and come),
No more a stranger or a guest, but like a child at home.*

In those moments, as the choir sang these powerful words, I began to go back in time and remember some of those who have experienced great tragedy, who "walked thru the valley of the shadow of death", yet in their darkest moments of life, found "a settled rest." They continued on in life, not just surviving, but living victoriously and with joy.

*© 2015 by Intellectual Reserve, Inc.

The Song Of Endurance

She was a meek older woman in the first church where I served as a pastor. She lived in a small white-framed home in the country surrounded by vast acreage filled with rolling hills, small ponds and lots of cattle. Every Sunday she would arrive and look for new people coming into the church to welcome them and direct them to either Sunday school or a pew in which to sit. Her blue eyes always had a twinkle in them, and her smile brought immediate peace and comfort. In short, she was the humble matriarch of the church.

In just a few weeks, I learned that she had tremendous tragedy in her life. After just eight years of marriage, she saw her husband killed as the tractor he was driving turned over on him, killing him instantly. She was left to raise four children on her own, three boys and a daughter. Within time, her oldest son died from cancer, her next son committed suicide and her youngest son was killed in the Vietnam War. Her daughter suffered from mental illness and was frequently in and out of mental care facilities. Nevertheless, she was always in worship. When she sang the great hymns of the faith her face seemed to have an aura of the holy around it. She was one of my favorite members!

In my third year as her pastor, I knew I would be moving away to be the pastor of another church. I called and asked her if I could visit her, and we set the time for the next early afternoon.

When I arrived, she was sitting on her front porch in a rocking chair. She stood up to give me a hug and then we sat down and chatted for a while. Finally, I said to her, "How do you do it? How do you live so triumphantly after having such deep tragedy: the loss of your husband, the deaths of all three sons and the mental issues of your daughter?"

She was quiet for a time, looking over the street to the pasture with cows eating the grass. Her blue eyes became shinier and she turned to me with words I have never forgotten. She said, "I have learned over the years that when you keep your eyes centered on Jesus Christ, you can endure anything."

Endurance meant staying focused on the life, ministry, teachings, death and resurrection of the One who suffered as we do, and yet overcame to offer us, and all the world, the gift of his presence. She never completed high school, she was never a professor of theology, or ordained to preach, but she spoke the good news of God's grace in a simple and profound way, and most powerfully, she lived it.

Another out of my past was a woman whose daughter was killed in a car accident on New Year's Eve on her way back to college that was out-of-state. A year later, her oldest son died of leukemia at age 18. Her youngest child, a daughter, was murdered four years later. She never missed church. She did not miss work. She kept going. She was named "Educator of the year" by her county educational system. Though retired now, she still tutors children and is active in her local church. She will always grieve the deaths of her beloved children, but God's presence in her life enables her to move forward and not to give up.

My mother lived thirty years with cancer, fifteen labeled "terminal" by her physicians. She was one who was raised by great parents, but close to poverty. She was too poor to finish college. She experienced the betrayal of a loved one that shattered her family and suffered from the emotional and physical pains of cancer. In spite of all of her trials and heartaches, mother was a person of deep faith and strong fortitude. She was the kind of person that drew people to her, and she was always willing to help. Her favorite hymn was the old gospel hymn "Others".

> "Lord help me live from today to day
> in such a self-forgetful way
> that even when I kneel to pray,
> my prayer will be for others."*

---

*Miegs, Charles D. "Others", 1915 public domain

The Song Of Endurance

She was a missionary to Belize, worked for Wesley Homes (a geriatric facility owned and operated by the United Methodist Church), and spent countless hours raising money for missions around the world.

Six months before her death, she danced at my daughter's wedding. No one would know how sick she was just a couple of hours before the service began. She would not let anything hinder her from living life to the fullest.

By her bed, on top of her Bible, her favorite poem could be found.

> **I've dreamed many dreams;**
> **that never came true**
> **I've seen them vanish at dawn**
> **But, I've realized enough of my dreams;**
> **to make me want to dream on**
>
> **I've prayed many prayers;**
> **and no answer came**
>
> **Tho' I waited patient and long**
> **But God has answered enough of my prayers;**
> **to keep me praying on**
>
> **I've drained the cup of disappointment and pain**
> **I've gone many a day without a song**
>
> **But, I have sipped enough nectar from the roses of life;**
> **to make me want to live on.***

---

*Greene, Ruth Parks. Steadfast Heart. 1918

I realize that this was one of God's songs to her. It is a song that empowered her to endure through the dark, through the night, to the light of eternal day.

Looking back through history there are many who experienced great pain and sorrow who "sipped enough nectar from the roses of life to make them want to live on."

Martin Luther King, Sr. lost his first son to a drowning accident, his second son to assassination and his wife was murdered in the church where he was the pastor and she was playing the organ on a Sunday morning. He would say following her death, "I am too old to start hating now, I'm going to keep on loving."

Barbara Bush lost a daughter at the age of 3 to leukemia. She had five more children and became the "grandmother of the nation." Deeply bereaved by her daughter's death, she heard God's song of endurance and kept on going.

Joe Biden's wife (and a daughter) died when his children were young. He raised them by himself while continuing his work in politics. A few years ago, his oldest son died. It was a monumental loss to him, and his tears flowed freely in interviews following the death. However, Joe kept on going. He completed his work as vice-president of the United States and now feels strong enough to run for the presidency of this country.

I wish my friend who took his life, had picked up the phone in his hour of despair and called a friend, gone to the hospital, or found someone to hold him until he once again had that "settled rest" and held on for life. It has been said of suicide that it is" a permanent solution to temporary issues." Had he called me; I would have been at his home in a flash. The world has lost a great man who had a tremendous mind, a giant heart and a passion for people. With all of my heart, I believe that if he could speak to us today, he would say, "Don't do what I did. Find help. Relief will come." I believe he would quote the psalmist who said, "weeping may tarry through the night, but joy comes in the morning." (Psalm 30)

The Song Of Endurance

Who are the ones in your life who have inspired you with faithful endurance? When crisis and tragedy come, listen for God's song of endurance. It will come in the night bringing new strength, purpose and light.

You shall have a song as in the night

Isaiah 30: 29 NRSV

Chapter 3

The Song of Generosity

*I*n my senior year of college, I applied to the Candler School of Theology of Emory University to enter seminary. When my acceptance letter came, I was shocked to read that I had received a scholarship that would pay for each year if I maintained a 3.5 academic average. Being a "book-worm" I thought this was doable.

Upon arriving on campus, I soon learned that seminary was not a monastery where we would spend the majority of our time in prayer, praise and worship. Though we had worship twice a week, seminary was graduate school with all that comes with that. The professors had stringent requirements for their classes and in addition to my studies, I had to work in a setting of ministry. I was assigned Children's Hospital at Egleston where I had to work as a chaplain ten-hours a week and be "on-call" one weekend a month for the first quarter.

In addition to my seminary responsibilities, I was an organist and youth minister for a church near my home. That meant Wednesday night choir practice, hours of practice, Sunday worship and Sunday evening with the youth. My "dance-card" was full to overflowing.

Songs In The Night

    The first quarter seemed to sail by and soon my second quarter began. It was even more packed because the courses I took required many hours outside of the classroom for colloquies and other placements for learning. Now I was working on the "terminal" cancer floor of Emory University Hospital ten hours a week and on-call once a month. Like a sponge, I soaked up everything I could in class and my assignments and responsibilities outside of them.

    By the time my first year was completed, I was mentally and physically exhausted. My grades seemed good enough to keep my scholarship. However, one week after classes ended, I received a phone call from the director of scholarships telling me I had lost my scholarship by .04 of a point! I was devastated! What would I do for money to pay the next two years? Would I have to drop out, work full-time and take one class a quarter? If so, that would mean I would be in seminary for many years.

    Immediately, I began to look for full-time summer work. I had few skills and was new to the Atlanta area, so I began to feel overwhelmed and somewhat sorry for myself. The organist position I had was an interim position while the organist of the church left to take a course in another state. She was back, and I was out of the job.

    A couple of days after receiving the news that I was without funds to go to seminary, my phone rang at home and a voice on the line said, "It is my understanding you need a job and I have one for you if you are interested." He told me that the Sunday-school teacher where I was attending worship had called him and told him I needed work. Without even knowing what the job entailed or the wages I would receive, I told him I was ready and able. I went to work the next day at a tool company in downtown Atlanta.

    The company was moving their business from Lucky Street to Marietta Street and needed extra help to move tools and clean up. My first job in this new setting was to empty every garbage can in

The Song Of Generosity

all 40 offices and sweep up from the day before in the new office building and then go to Lucky Street for the remainder of the day.

The people I got to know were wonderful to me. Soon I felt like a chaplain to most of the employees, and they were kind and gracious to me. We worked together for three months, until my summer ended, and I was to return to Emory.

I knew that I did not make enough to pay for a full quarter at Emory and had decided to apply for a student loan. I did not want to accumulate large student debts, but I had no choice.

When I returned to my parent's home, there was a letter waiting for me. It was from Emory University. I dreaded opening it for fear tuition had escalated and my tuition due earlier than expected.

Slowly I opened it and when I finished reading the letter, I had to sit down. I could not believe my eyes. The letter said that an anonymous donor had paid for my next two years in seminary!!!! I read and reread it over and over in total shock and joy. Naturally, I was curious to know who would do such a thing. Who knew I needed the help? I did not share with anyone about losing my scholarship outside of my immediate family.

Later that day when we sat down to eat, I told my folks that I was amazed by this person's generosity. It was the biggest gift I had ever received. I would need to write this person(s) a thank you note and give it to the university to give it to them since it was anonymous.

We spent time talking about the generosity of the anonymous giver and then my father, in his great wisdom, said to me: "you will need to write more thank you notes than that one because there have been many who have been generous toward you this summer: your Sunday school teacher, the president of the company who hired you, the people you have gotten to know there, as well as this anonymous person. I had not stopped to think about that. Basically, I had felt that only one person had been generous to me, but that was not so.

Dad was in the mood to talk about how much we had all received through the church. He continued on saying that I would not be at Emory if it were not for the United Methodist Church and all the people who gave generously over many years for it to exist. And what about the medical center at Emory and all the research being accomplished for the well-being of other's health.

The discussion continued as we began to think about all it took to make one day possible with the things we enjoyed: those who built houses, made furniture, farmers, newspaper writers, printers, and the paper carrier; radio and television stations providing entertainment, the postal worker bringing our mail each day, the workers who claimed our garbage, cleaned our streets, and police and firefighters who gave us security. On and on we went, and the list became longer and longer. I became acutely aware of the blessings that were mine.

Interestingly, I am still learning that generosity is not always in "big" ways, but in small ways from "big" hearts. When my grandchildren pick a flower in the yard and rush to bring it to me, they are thrilled to give it and my heart swells with love for them in their act of generosity. A simple act with profound meaning beyond words!

One of the greatest true stories of generosity I have ever heard was how Temple University came into being. It began from the piggy bank of a seven-year-old girl named Hattie May Wiatt in 1884. She was from a poor home near Philadelphia, Pennsylvania. A new pastor of the local Baptist church (Rev. Russell Conwell) was such an accomplished preacher that the church began to grow to the point that soon people had to have a ticket to come to Sunday school and worship due to lack of space. (soon it got to where tickets had to be obtained weeks in advance)

The pastor could see that many children stood outside trying to get into Sunday school and worship and were turned away. One day, little Hattie May Wyatt came with her books and a contribution to go to Sunday school. She stood outside the gate trying to

The Song Of Generosity

decide whether to wait or go back home. Her clothes were ragged, and she was unkempt. The pastor's heart went out to her and he walked to the gate, picked her up and took to the classroom and found a chair for her in the corner of the room.

The next morning the pastor passed her house as he walked to the church. He saw her outside and said, "Hattie, when we get the money, we are going to build a bigger church where all the children have room to come to Sunday school and worship."

When she did not show up for a couple of Sundays, he went to her home and discovered that she was very sick. He went and sat by her bed and had prayer with her. She reached under her pillow and retrieved some coins and gave them to the pastor saying "this is the money I have saved for you to build that bigger church. Take it and build a place where all of us kids have room to go."

Within a few days, Hattie died. She had saved 57 cents. Her mother brought it to the church and gave it to the pastor. The next Sunday, he stood in the pulpit and told Hattie's story. He exchanged her coins for 57 pennies and laid them on the altar. At the end of the service people began to go the altar and leave an offering in exchange for a penny. By the end of the service there was enough money to buy the house north of the church where the primary Sunday school class could enlarge. The Wiatt Mite Society was formed. From there, monies began to flow, and soon more property was purchased and soon there was a new sanctuary, new education center, and the house bought with the original funds from the service where Hattie's pennies were put on the altar, became the origin of Temple University.

Visitors at Temple can see a portrait of Hattie May Wiatt as they enter the campus. From the generosity of a child's 57 cents and the blessing of God, not only was a new church formed, but a great university with one of the finest medical centers in the world.

The only miracle of Jesus that appears in all four gospels is the feeding of the 5000. Though all tell it, John's gospel is the only one that shares about a little boy who gives his lunch bag to Jesus containing two loaves and five fish. Jesus takes it and blesses it, and all ate and were satisfied. We are told that there were twelve baskets of food left over!!! (if we try to figure this out, we lose the meaning of the passage: miracles can happen when we offer what we have to God.)

Throughout my life, I have been blessed by numerous people who have given what they had for God to bless and the miracle of miracles is that multitudes of people have been blessed. These blessings have flowed into the community, the state and around the world, bringing hope, food, medical aid in times of crisis, and provided education for many.

When my sister was a missionary to Nicaragua, she worked on a small island called Puerto Cabasis. This was a small town where transportation there could only be by plane or boat. When a military coup occurred in the capital city of Managua, many of the injured were flown to the Moravian hospital where she was a nurse. To her surprise, medical supplies came in boxes from the United Methodist Committee on Relief, an organization where 100% of funds given go to help people in crisis all over the world. (UMCOR can be anywhere in the world in four hours-time bringing relief.) Without the generosity of people, the church could not be so involved. Overwhelmed that her church really did what it said it did, when she returned to the states, she spent time traveling to various churches speaking on behalf of UMCOR.

As a pastor, I have had people say to me that they had little to give toward a mission, a building project, or the general offerings of the church. My response is always the same; give what you can and offer it to God. It will multiply. Generosity always blesses.

There have been times in my own life when I did not think I could make ends meet financially. The needs of my family were too great. Many a night the darkness enfolded me in fear. Often, the song of God through one of my mother's favorite hymns would

The Song Of Generosity

come to mind and I would focus on all of my blessings rather than what I didn't have. That hymn goes like this:

> When upon life's billows you are tempest-tossed,
> When you are discouraged, thinking all is lost,
> Count your many blessings, name them one by one,
> And it will surprise you what the Lord has done.

Refrain:

> Count your blessings, name them one by one,
> Count your blessings, see what God has done!
> Count your blessings, name them one by one,
> Count your many blessings, see what God has done.
> And it will surprise you what the Lord has done.
>
> Are you ever burdened with a load of care?
> Does the cross seem heavy you are called to bear?
> Count your many blessings, every doubt will fly,
> And you will keep singing as the days go by.
>
> When you look at others with their lands and gold,
> Think that Christ has promised you His wealth untold;
> Count your many blessings—*money cannot buy [*wealth can never buy]
> Your reward in heaven, nor your home on high.
>
> So, amid the conflict whether great or small,
> Do not be discouraged, God is over all;
> Count your many blessings, angels will attend,
> Help and comfort give you to your journey's end.*

*Oatman, Jr., Johnson. "Count Your Many Blessings. 1987

Whenever I am feeling discouraged and "down", when my finances are stretched to the limit from multitudes of necessities: braces for my children's teeth, medical care, car upkeep, maintenance on the house, taxes, insurance, college tuition, clothing, food and everything else that are needed for basic living in todays world, I stop and try to remember to take a deep breath and count, not my losses, but my gains.

I can remember an older man in the first church where I worked as a youth pastor while I was in seminary. He was a brilliant attorney who was retired and in his upper 80's. Sometimes after I preached on Sunday evening, he would come up to me with his hand out to shake my hand and inside of his would be a $20.00 bill. He would whisper where no one could hear him, "use this for gas or your expenses." One day, he came to my office carrying a brown paper bag. He sat down and said to me that he loved the commentaries of William Barclay. He told me how much they had meant to him in his personal devotions and in teaching Sunday school. He stood up and said, "Hope you can get as much out of them as I have." He left.

I went to the bag and in there was a brand-new set of the Barclay Commentaries. That was over 40 years ago, and I still have them and use them almost weekly.

There are those who have let me go first in the grocery line, let me get in front of them in heavy traffic, people who have sent cards, brought food for no reason but to be kind.

But it doesn't stop there. As I have been blessed, I realize that my response is to be a blessing to others. I vowed when I received the letter telling me that an anonymous donor had paid for my last two years of seminary, that I would always contribute to my colleges and universities where I have attended. Giving my first 10% of my income to the church allows me to be one who can help make dreams come true for others. My offerings above that, can bless even more as I seek to give to colleges, children's homes, and other missional needs.

Before my parents died, my siblings and I decided to honor them by making it possible to have a scholarship in their names to the colleges where they began their first year. Dad's was to Young Harris College, and mothers was to Reinhardt University. Since their deaths, some thirty youth have had scholarships making it possible for them to attend college.

It is my goal to work toward scholarships for needy students at the colleges and universities that I attended. I am reminded that all the colleges and universities, churches, children's homes, facilities for the elderly, facilities for the disabled, and the multitude of ministries through the church would not be possible without all of the unnamed persons who gave and who continue to give generously. We are all the recipients of the generosity of others!

And what of the generosity of God! The gift of a world full of beautiful terrain, creatures, and human life. There are hundreds of galaxies like ours, the sun, the moon, the stars, the oceans, the mountains, the winds and rain. Each day is a new creation from the creator.

God's great gift in Jesus Christ is the greatest act of generosity: the ability to be forgiven, redeemed, made whole and given new life, eternal life that begins even now. We are a people who have been given the world! Literally! We are all wealthy when it comes to being showered with God's great love for us.

I have been with those who have found themselves in jail, or in the throws of a bitter divorce, or received the news that they have a debilitating illness that will ultimately cause their deaths, or the loss of a job and the possibility of bankruptcy, who cry out, "Does anyone care?" "I feel all alone." Darkness seems to cover them, and they feel little hope. My words to them are always, "Hold on." The darkness will not last forever. Let's look at what you do have." Then we begin to name the things that we often forget and realize the blessings that are ours.

Songs In The Night

The song of generosity is the song of remembering who we are and whose we are. We have a future, a great future, because we are never alone. God is with us in this very moment and always.

I would encourage us all, when the darkness comes our way, to stop and remember the songs of generosity. It has many tunes and words.

> Fear not I am with thee, O be not dismayed
> For I am your God and will still give you aid
> I will strengthen and help you and cause you to stand
> Upheld by my righteous, omnipotent hand.*
>
> O lord my God, when I in awesome wonder
> Consider all, the worlds Thy hands have made
> I see the stars, I hear the rolling thunder
> Thy power throughout, the universe displayed
>
> Then sings my soul, my savior God to Thee
> How Great thou art!
>
> When through the woods, and forest glades I wander
> And hear the birds sing sweetly in the trees
> When I look down from lofty mountain grandeur
> And hear the brook and feel the gentle breeze.
> Then sings my soul.....my savior God to thee.
>
> The Bible tells the story of your blessing
> So freely shed upon all human life;
> Your constant mercy, every care addressing,
> relieving burdened souls from sin and strife.
> Then sings my soul....my savior God to thee.

*Rippon, John. "How Firm a Foundation" 1787. UMH

The Song Of Generosity

And when at last, the clouds of doubt dispersing,
You will reveal what we but dimly see;
With trumpet call, our great rebirth announcing,
we shall rejoin you for eternity.
Then sings my soul....my savior God to thee!*

When we remember the generosity of God and of others, the darkness begins to fade into the light, and we can but sing "How Great Thou Art! How great Thou art!

In the night God's song shall be with us and the song of generosity is one of God's favorites.

*Hine, Stuart K. "How Great Thou Art". 1949. UMH

God is my strength and my song.

Isaiah 12:2 NRSV

CHAPTER 4

The Song of Community

Several years ago, a wonderful couple in the church where I was serving, had their second child, a son. He was born with a neuromuscular disease. He could not use his arms or legs nor lift his head. The doctors were not hopeful that he would ever be able to use them. The child's mother was not content with this prognosis. She began to study everything she could about his health problem. She called other physicians, took him to various clinics and finally decided it was up to her to make this child well. She began to work daily with his arms and legs. By the time he was thirteen months old, he was able to lift his arms and legs. Doctors were amazed.

The child's neck was still limp. Nevertheless, she worked diligently to make him stronger. Little by little, progress was being made until he came down with a cold. For a person who cannot lift the head to have a cold can be deadly. The cold turned into pneumonia. He went to Children's Hospital at Egleston in the Intensive Care Unit. Certainly, after all the progress he had made, it would be tragic for him to take a major backset. The entire community began praying for him. Churches from all over the county were having special praying services for him. He had been in ICU over a month.

He began to worsen, and the doctors felt a tracheotomy was necessary for him to live. The mother knew that if that happened, his ability to lift his neck would be next to impossible. She begged the doctors to hold off.

Amazingly, he began to heal. The tracheotomy was not performed. Within a few days he would be able to come home from the hospital. The community was ecstatic.

The mother called me and told me they would come home from the hospital on the Wednesday of Holy Week. She asked if she could speak to the church on Sunday and thank them for all they did for their family and especially their son. I said, "That would be awesome." I was thrilled to have a miracle like the one that had just happened, celebrated on Easter Sunday.

On Good Friday, the mother took her son to get a haircut, so he would look his best for Easter. While driving from their home to the barbershop, a sixteen year-old-girl, high on drugs, came around a curve on the wrong side of the road, hitting the mother and son head-on. The baby was killed instantly, and the mother had broken ribs, punctured lungs, and a smashed spleen. She was air-flighted to the nearest hospital for emergency surgery. Upon hearing of this news, I rushed to the hospital to be there for her and the family. After several hours of surgery, she finally came into the recovery room. Her first words were "How is my baby?" The doctors, nurses, her husband and parents were teary. I stepped toward her and took her hand and told her that her son did not make it. The grief on her face was beyond words. We were all in shock and deeply bereaved.

The funeral had to be delayed for ten days in order for the mother to be released from the hospital and to get home and heal enough to make the service. I knew the community would come out in large numbers because we had all come together to pray for this little one. Our hearts were heavy. It seemed like a black cloud hovered over our community.

The Song Of Community

My wife was expecting our second child at the time, and I could not imagine losing one that I loved this much. Every time I tried to work on the eulogy for this little boy, the tears flowed down my face. The words would not come. Finally, I went to my Bible Study group and told them I was having tremendous trouble with all of this. I opened my heart and shared my soul. They said to me, "When you get up to deliver the eulogy, you look at us. We will be holding you up in prayer and you will find the strength to do this." We all hugged and prayed together.

On the day of the funeral, the church was packed to capacity and we even had an overflow room filled with folks watching the service via close-circuit television. The family was sitting right in front of me. Seeing the eyes of the mother and father of that little boy caused a huge knot in my throat. Looking out over the congregation and seeing the multitudes with tears streaming down their faces gave me feelings of panic. We all needed a word of grace. We were there to be comforted and to find peace in the midst of deepest grief.

Finally, the time came for me to stand and walk to the pulpit to deliver the eulogy. I stood there and looked over the congregation and saw my Bible study group sitting together. They were sitting up together with smiles on their faces mouthing to me "you can do it."

When I began to speak, the voice I had was not my regular voice! It was deep and calm and smooth. It was like I was speaking yet someone else doing the talking. I had never experienced anything like it before or after.

When the service was over, and I was outside waiting for the family to gather into their automobiles to head to the cemetery, several came up to me and remarked on my voice. I heard things like, "your voice gave us the assurance we needed" or "how did you have such a strong voice in the midst of your own deep sadness?"

I could call it the work of the Holy Spirit. I could call it the result of prayer. Most of all, I would call it a mystery. What I did learn from that is that when the community shares in our grief, by praying, enfolding us in their arms and care, and by being there for us, we are equipped to go forward. We can walk "through" the valley to the other side, into the light.

In short, we need community. Jesus knew the vital importance of community and that is why he gave the world the church. There are those who do not attend a church or religious organization who say they are "spiritual but not religious." I have known people who say that they are "saved" but have no interest in the church. My response to them is "who do you think gave you the Bible? Who do you think began the church? Did you realize that Christianity is not a religion but a relationship with Jesus Christ who we know best in the community of faith?" I have found that some of these who love God, but not the church, are fine with their attitudes until there is a tragedy or crisis. The first call they make is to a church for a pastor to perform a funeral or to come to the hospital or institution of chemical dependency. And thanks be to God the church is there for them!

When I am overcome by crisis, tragedy or despair, it is to the church that I turn. True, it is not perfect because it is made up of humans, but it is the closet thing to heaven on earth.

It is the church that began the first institution of higher education in the United States (Harvard), the importance of hospitals, children's homes, places for the elderly, institutions for the chemically addicted, and equips missionaries to go all over the world to help feed, clothe and teach the needy.

During the campaign to build an education facility in the church where I was serving, a grandmother in the community who was raising her two grandchildren, lost her home to fire. She had no insurance. She was a nurse in one of the elementary schools in the county and beloved by many. The fire happened on a Friday night destroying everything she owned.

The Song Of Community

On Sunday morning as I was getting robed and ready for the 11:00 worship service, some members from one of the adult Sunday school classes came into my office sharing the news about the fire and their class's decision to build her a new home in one day! They wanted the whole church to participate.

I wanted to help, but knew money was tight. How on earth could we afford to build her a new home and even crazier, in one day!!! Nevertheless, a called meeting of the church council was held, and it was a unanimous vote to do this.

The following Saturday morning at 7:00am, I stood on a cement foundation that had been poured the day before and had a prayer as 80+ people from the church and the community came together to build the miracle house in one day!

Word had seeped out in the community and soon people came to watch, bring food, and offer their services. Within a few hours, strangers became new friends. We worked diligently all day and at 7:00pm, shutters were being put on the windows! The electrical work would be done on Monday, and the family could move in by the next Saturday. All who were there witnessed the miracle of a house being built in one day!

The next day, Sunday morning, there were new faces in the congregation. People who had come from the surrounding area who saw the work of the church and community wanted to be in the fellowship of those who cared enough to act for the benefit of one in greatest need.

Without the community of faith, we are left to wallow aimlessly in our own thoughts and beliefs. This can be very dangerous.

Near the end of my college days, I felt I needed to take an education course to help me in learning to teach in the church. The professor gave out the syllabus and some of our "labs" were on Wednesday evenings. After class, I went to her and said, "I need to talk with you about the Wednesday labs because for the next month I am filling in as organist of First United Methodist Church in the

Songs In The Night

downtown area near the college." She said, "Oh how wonderful! I want to come hear you." I was not expecting that response. I then asked her, "Where do you go to church?" She said, "I don't go to church. I stay home and read my Bible and wherever it talks of God as light I underline that in yellow, when it talks of sin, I underline that in black, and when it talks of grace, I underline that in green." She continued on, "I have a daughter that has down-syndrome and have to stay home with her. God punished me with her because I had her when I was not married."

I was not in seminary, but I knew there was something wrong with that last statement. Does God punish someone else for our mistakes? What does that say about God? Jesus talks about God being like the good parent and no good parent would do something that horrible to a child. More than anything, this woman needed a community of faith that could help her expand her thinking and help her to know that God does not act like that. If God is love, then love seeks the best.

I will never forget the morning I parked my car and entered the church where I was the pastor. To my surprise the hallway was packed with people watching a television that had been rolled out of a classroom. One the screen it showed planes flying directly into the twin towers in New York City. We watched in horror. America had been invaded on our own soil!

We watched as images of the Pentagon came into focus. Another plane had hit it, and another crashed in Pennsylvania that was headed for Washington, D.C to destroy the nation's capital. No one could move as we tried to absorb what was happening.

Immediately I called the clergy together and we began to plan a service for that evening. With such little notice, it was difficult to get the word out to the community.

At 7:00 that same evening, the sanctuary was filled to capacity and people stood in the back and around the side aisles. We were a nation in great pain and fear and churches all over the country were packed. Everyone needed a place and a people to help move forward. The church has the message of grace, eternal peace and the message of redemption and forgiveness. The very cross is the symbol that God can take a disaster and transform it into a means of grace and salvation.

As I looked out over the crowd that evening, I thought to myself that "spiritual but not religious" does not work. We need to be together. We need the assurance that only the community of faith can give.

The opening hymn that evening was one that I had never sung, but it was amazingly appropriate for all who gathered together:

> For the healing of the nations,
> Lord, we pray with one accord,
> for a just and equal sharing
> of the things that earth affords.
> To a life of love in action
> help us rise and pledge our word.
>
> Lead us forward into freedom,
> from despair your world release,
> that, redeemed from war and hatred,
> all may come and go in peace.
> Show us how through care and goodness
> fear will die and hope increase.
>
> All that kills abundant living,
> let it from the earth be banned:
> pride of status, race or schooling,
> dogmas that obscure your plan.
> In our common quest for justice
> may we hallow brief life's span.

> You, Creator God, have written
> your great name on humankind;
> for our growing in your likeness
> bring the life of Christ to mind;
> that by our response and service
> earth its destiny may find.*

At the end of the service we sang a familiar hymn that everyone could sing without having to look at the words that seemed to say it all:

This little light of mine, I'm gonna let it shine. All through the night, I'm gonna let it shine. Let it shine, let it shine, let it shine.**

That is what we needed, to see the light and to be the light in a world that had suddenly gone dark on us. The community of faith was such a light that evening when all the eyes of the world were looking at us to know how we would respond to such horrible acts of hate and destruction. By ourselves we can grow cynical and full of bitterness and anger leading to more destruction of ourselves and others. More than ever, the world needs the church's message of love, peace and forgiveness to light the way to a world that reflects more of what God had in mind in creation.

I am reminded of the old hymn from my childhood that we sang each Sunday evening as we completed youth group:

> Blest be the tie that binds
> Our hearts in Christian love;
> The fellowship of kindred minds
> Is like to that above.

---

*Kaan, Fred. "For the Healing of the Nations." Hope Publishing Company, 1965. UMN
**Curnow, Jim. "This little light of mine". Plank Road Publishing, Ink. UMH

The Song Of Community

> Before our Father's throne,
> We pour our ardent prayers;
> Our fears, our hopes, our aims are one,
> Our comforts, and our cares.
>
> We share our mutual woes,
> Our mutual burdens bear;
> And often for each other flows
> The sympathizing tear.
>
> When we asunder part,
> It gives us inward pain;
> But we shall still be joined in heart,
> And hope to meet again.*

Every time I hear it, I am reminded of all of us who stood in a circle holding hands singing that great hymn and the feeling of being a part of a larger family. I sensed that I belonged. I knew I was not alone. It was our theme song that united us and filled us with hope and peace.

For many years the hymn *Lift Every Voice and Sing* has been considered the Black National Anthem. It brings a sense of unity, belonging and hope. During the years of slavery, it was their churches that brought hope, strength and courage. Dr. Martin Luther King, Jr., grew up under the ministry of his father in Ebenezer Baptist Church in Atlanta, Georgia. Later he would become pastor to Dexter Avenue Baptist church in Montgomery, Alabama, where he began the civil rights movement in 1956. Long before King began the march for equal rights for all people, James Weldon Johnson and J. Rosamond Johnson wrote the words and music to *Lift Every Voice and Sing* in 1921, where it was sung in churches across America. Its words are stirring and profound:

*Fawcett, John. "Blest be the tie that Binds." 1740-1817 UMH

Songs In The Night

Lift Every Voice and Sing

Lift every voice and sing, till earth and Heaven ring,
Ring with the harmonies of liberty;
Let our rejoicing rise, high as the listening skies,
Let it resound loud as the rolling sea.
Sing a song full of the faith that the dark past has taught us,
Sing a song full of the hope that the present has brought us;
Facing the rising sun of our new day begun,
Let us march on till victory is won.

Stony the road we trod, bitter the chastening rod,
Felt in the days when hope unborn had died;
Yet with a steady beat, have not our weary feet,
Come to the place for which our fathers sighed?
We have come over a way that with tears has been watered,
We have come, treading our path
through the blood of the slaughtered;
Out from the gloomy past, till now we stand at last
Where the white gleam of our bright star is cast.

God of our weary years, God of our silent tears,
Thou Who hast brought us thus far on the way;
Thou Who hast by Thy might, led us into the light,
Keep us forever in the path, we pray.
Lest our feet stray from the places, our God, where we met Thee.
Lest our hearts, drunk with the wine of the world, we forget Thee.
Shadowed beneath Thy hand, may we forever stand,
True to our God, true to our native land.*

---

*Johnson, Rosamond J., and James Weldon Johnson. "Lift every voice and Sing."
Edwards B. Marks Music Company/Shawnee Press Inc. 1900 UMH

The Song Of Community

Without the church, the civil rights movement would not have begun.

A few years ago, a couple in the church where I served lost both of their sons in a car accident. One was 33 the other 31. In one quick moment their children were gone. The Sunday following their funerals, they were in worship. When I went to greet them, they said, "where else can we find the strength we need to live today and face tomorrow." That is what the church offers: strength and courage for today and hope for tomorrow.

Whenever the darkness of aloneness sweeps over me and I feel so small and insignificant, I remember the church that lifts us beyond ourselves to work together toward a higher goal for all of humanity to have faith, hope, love and a peace that the world does not understand, but only comes through the "body" of Christ, His church. He is the one who gave us the church in the first place. It is His creation. It is his "bride" so to speak. He gave his life for it. Therefore, we must never take it lightly. Indeed, we must care for it like our own body.

When we respond to the invitation of the church to be loyal with our prayers, presence, gifts, service and witness for Christ, we will find ourselves humming another of God's songs in the night, the song of community.

'Where is God my Maker,
who gives songs in the night,

Job 35:10 NRSV

Chapter 5

The Song of Example

One of the requirements when I was in seminary was having to participate in a clinical internship for a whole quarter. For forty hours a week, I was a chaplain at Budd Terrace, one of the care centers at Wesley Woods, a geriatric facility owned and operated by the United Methodist Church.

My first day on the job, I went to the nurse's station on the second floor of Budd Terrace and asked the head nurse where I should begin my duties. She paused a minute and said, "Go to the last room at the end of the hall. The woman there lost her husband of seventy years a few weeks ago and she could use some cheering up."

I made my way down the long hallway and knocked on the last door. A voice on the inside said, "come in." She was sitting in a chair, dressed in a housecoat and bedroom slippers. I introduced myself and she told me her name and age. She was 97 years old. I referred to her as Ms. R.

I sat down and let her tell me about the recent loss of her husband. As she talked about her family, I realized that I knew her granddaughter. I asked her, "was your granddaughter Miss Georgia a few years ago?" She said, "That's correct." I told her my father had been her pastor when she was a little girl. Small world we both said out loud!

After about an hour of visiting with her I told her I would come back and visit again soon. She said, "Don't go yet! I don't want you to think I am some old lady who is washed up and depressed. Let me tell you what happened to me last week."

She told me that at Budd Terrace if a resident has to leave the facility, they had to have a partner to go with them. She needed to do some banking and so she and her 99-year-old friend caught the special Marta bus and went to the Trust Company Bank across the street from Emory University. She did her banking quickly and then the two of them walked across the street at the busy intersection of North Decatur Road and Clifton Road. They walked to the bench in front of the Gambrell School of Law at Emory to wait for the bus to return and pick them up.

It was a scorching hot August afternoon. She did not want her friend to get too warm and pass out, so she looked around for something to block the sun. She saw a piece of cardboard that would work so she brought over to the bench and held it up to block the sun.

People passing by would smile and point at them as they passed by. She remarked to her friend, "My, isn't the world getting friendlier these days!"

They waited and two young law students walking across the campus of the law school saw them and doubled over laughing. She turned to her friend and said, "I guess this does look funny; two old women sitting in front of a law school."

From a distance she saw the bus coming their way, so she stood up. Not wanting to litter and thinking someone would come after them to sit on the bench in the heat, she decided to leave the cardboard on the bench. When she turned the cardboard over, to her shock, the words on the other side said: FOR SALE!

I laughed until I thought I would cry. We both laughed. I fell in love with this woman!

Every Tuesday and Thursday morning at 10:00, I would have a devotional in the main room on the second floor. I began to notice that on both of those mornings I would see Ms. R. coming out of her room around 9:00 and knock on doors. The residents would open their doors and she would ask them about their health, their family and then remind them that the "little" chaplain would be holding devotions at 10:00 and they would not want to miss.

She walked the entire length of the hallway knocking on doors. One day I stopped her and asked her what she was doing. She said, "I am shaking the bushes." I told her I didn't know what that meant. She said, "How do you think you get people to attend devotions each time you have them? Most of the residents here can't remember who they are much less who you are. It is my ministry to let them know."

At 97-years of age she was still working for God! She taught me that we never retire from serving God. She was an example to me of a Christ-like life.

My grandmother was similar to Ms. R. She moved into a nursing home at the age of 90. Every Monday morning, she would call the church she had attended for 70 years and asked them for the updated "concern" list. She would spend the morning calling each person and listen to what was wrong and then she would have prayer for them. After her lunch, she would go up and down the hallways of the facility in her wheelchair visiting those who were sick or lonely. She never retired from serving God; another example of a Christ-like life.

In one of the churches from my past, there was a woman who was in charge of the preschool of the church during the week and in charge of the nursey and primary area of the church on Sundays. During my time there, I do not remember her ever missing a Sunday.

I would learn that she was the national president of the Kenny Rogers Fan Club! She has attended over 1000 concerts all over

America, Europe and beyond. There were times she would fly to London for a concert on Saturday evening and fly back all night, so she could be at the nursery on Sunday morning!

Going further back in my ministry, there was a couple who loved to camp. They would leave after work on Friday and camp through Sunday evening. No matter where they were, they would get up early on Sunday morning and drive back for Sunday school and worship.

The same with a Sunday School teacher I had while in my first year of seminary. She and her husband had a home on Lake Burton, but they lived in College Park, Georgia. She never missed a Sunday teaching the class. They would go up to the lake on Friday and come home early Sunday morning, so she would be ready to teach.

All of these are examples, models of a Christ-like life.

What kind of models are we? Do we "walk our talk of faith?" When we take the vows of church membership, do we strive to live up to them? Do we treat all we meet as if we are meeting Christ?

Many years I was at a college football game. I worked my way out of the row I was on to get something for my wife and me to drink. When I got near the concession stand, I heard a man cussing with great anger. His team was losing, and he was angry with the referees. As I walked closer toward him, I recognized him. He was a member of the church where I was pastor. He was a leader in the church! When he saw me, his face turned bright red and he hung his head. He came to me and said, "I am sorry you heard that." I was not sure he was sorry he had the cussing rampage, but only sorry I had heard him."

It is rare that I call myself a "Christian" because that term somehow means that we have "arrived." Rather, I am a Christian-in-the-making. Maybe a better way of putting it is that I am a "Christian-under-construction." Every day I try to live what I say I believe. It is never easy. Too often there are situations with people that test my ability to treat them as Christ. I don't think I am all alone here. How do we react when:

- A person cuts in line in front of us at a store?
- A person cuts us off on the highway?
- A child continues to do the things we have forbidden?
- A neighbor continually complains about the dog?
- The boss makes us work on holidays?

How do we treat someone when we are angry at them? I have often said that before we call ourselves Christian, we should ask those in our workplaces, neighborhoods, and family how we act when angry. One of the greatest examples of a Christ-like life are those who become angry but (as the Bible says) do not sin.

My wife and I tried to teach our children that it is okay to feel anger. Anger is a God-given feeling. However, it is not okay to act bad when angry. It is not okay to yell, hit, or hurt anyone.

A great example of this happened when I was appointed to begin a new church. After six months of taking in members, the time came for the church to hire an architect, buy land, and move from the dilapidated old schoolhouse where we were meeting (and renting) into something more permanent. We acquire ten acres. We hired the architect and formed a building committee. After five months of planning, the drawings were ready for the church to see and to vote on to get started. A church conference was held. The room was packed. There was excitement and anticipation about seeing the drawings. The architect showed what he had done, taking his time to point out what and why the design was a certain way.

After an hour of presentation, he opened the floor for questions. Only two men voiced major concerns. One was particularly angry. He did not think the present drawings encompassed what the church needed. He was concerned that there was no basement or drive-through. He asked dozens of questions all from negative reactions to what he had seen. The vote was taken. It was unanimous with the exception of two; those two men.

Songs In The Night

I was standing in the back of the room when the vote was taken. As soon as it was counted, the man who had raised the most questions stood and put on his coat and walked toward the door. I went to him and asked him if he was okay. He turned to me and said, "Do you think I am leaving because the vote did not go my way? I am a diabetic and need to get home to have my insulin. This is my church and I will respect the vote of the whole body. Tomorrow I will have you a check for $10,000 to get this project underway."

I stood there in utter shock and amazement as I watched him get in his car to go home. True to his word, the next day he left an envelope containing a $10,000 check to the church on my front door. When the building was near completion, he purchased all the pews for the sanctuary (at a considerable amount of money). He was one of the largest givers to the church and rarely missed a Sunday. He was an example of a Christ-like life.

Some of my heroes of living a Christ-like life are:

Martin Luther – he stood tall against the injustice of his church. He was persecuted and there were those who tried to kill him. He began the protestant revolution.

Rosa Parks – she was tired of injustice to her people. Instead of giving her seat to a white man on the bus, she refused and said she was tired. She was arrested, but her actions helped begin the civil rights movement.

Desmond Tutu- archbishop in South Africa who worked for the elimination of apartheid.

Martin Luther King, Jr.-
In the midst of persecution and hate, Martin Luther King, Jr., stood for nonviolent change.

The Song Of Example

Mother Teresa – leaving the comforts of life behind her, she moved to Calcutta, India, to give her life to help the poorest of the world to die with dignity. She began the Sisters of Charity that is now all over the world.

Pope John Paul II – who went to the prison and prayed with the man who shot him in an attempt to murder him. He offered words of love and forgiveness.

Ryan White – diagnosed with AIDS from a blood transfusion at an early age in his life. His neighbors, friends, and school all tried to banish him from their presence. He was treated like a leper. Not once did he retaliate with ugly words or actions. He kept on going. Soon he was a national figure for the fight against AIDS. Elton John sang at his funeral and from Ryan's example, John began a foundation to raise money for the elimination of AIDS and today that figure is in the millions of dollars.

There are many more who have borne the pains of tragedy, persecution and disease who have stood tall and never let hate or pain keep them from loving and caring for others. Their lives are examples of the one who on the cross prayed for those who betrayed him, nailed him to the tree, and forgave them. He is the greatest example of all.

There have been times when I have been wronged by someone. There have been times when people have said ugly things to me and behind my back. There have been times when I have gone the second mile for a person only to be "stabbed in the back" and mistreated. Many a night I have tossed and turned wanting to get back at those who hurt me, and then God's song comes to me in the night; the song of example, and I remember those who have stood tall in the midst persecution, injustice and abuse and triumphed by remaining steadfast to a higher calling. They did not react with hate

Songs In The Night

and hostility, but with dignity and kindness. As I remember I am able to calm down, to rest, and to try once more to know when to speak and when to remain silent, when to act and when not to act, and to strive to be one who treats others as Christ.

In the night, God's song comes to us and one of God's songs is the song of example.

My Song in The Night

O Jesus my Savior, my song in the night,
Come to us with Thy tender love,
my soul's delight.
Unto Thee, O Lord, in affliction I call,
My comfort by day, and my song in the night.

O why should I wander, an alien from Thee,
Or cry in the desert Thy face to see?
My comfort and joy, my soul's delight,
O Jesus my Savior, my song in the night.

My song in the night, my song in the night,
in the night, in the night, in the night.

My song my song in the night,
in the night, my song
My comfort and joy, my soul's delight.
O Jesus my savior, my song in the night,
in the night. My song in the night.*

---

*Wilberg, Mark. "My Song In the Night." American Folk Song. Mormon Tabernacle Choir

CHAPTER 6

The Song of Laughter

This might seem odd, but one of God's songs in the dark is the song of laughter.

One of my favorite movies is Steel Magnolias. It is the story of a group of women who are very close and they all center around one of them M'Lynn (Sally Field) who has a daughter named Shelby (Julia Roberts) who is severely diabetic. They journey with her through the festivies of her wedding, the birth of a son and the diagnosis that she is dying and her death. After the graveside service and people are leaving, M'Lynn begins to rant and rave at God about losing her beloved "Shelby". She walks around yelling, crying, arms flaying up and down in deep anger and grief. She shouts, "I am so angry I want to hit something." Clairee (Olympia Dukakis) surprises everyone when she pulls Ouiser (Shirley McClain) by the arm and says to M'Lynn, "Hit her. Come on, hit her. Everyone wants an opportunity to hit Ouiser." All of a sudden M'Lynn bursts out laughing. All of them begin to laugh (except Ouiser who huffs off angry). It was the laughter that broke into the darkness of M'Lynn's life causing her to see light and joy in the midst of deepest grief. Clariee had to do something to break the power of darkness." Laughter was just what M'Lynn needed in the midst of her deepest grief.

In my early years in ministry, I had a beloved member who was 89 years old and one of the saints of the church. I loved to visit her and sit on her front porch. She would reminisce about going to church in a horse-drawn wagon and how marvelous it was to see a man walk on the moon. She was a delight.

One day she said to me, "Pastor, you will officiate at my funeral. Here is what I want: tell people about the love of Jesus and leave them laughing." Interestingly, she died on Halloween (which was a Sunday morning) in her rocking chair watching the television show "Gospel Singing Jubilee".

At her funeral I told about three or four of the funniest things about her. The congregation delighted in them with the exception of her nieces and nephews. They sat stoned faced on the front row, never cracking a smile. Afterwards, they came to me and told me I had been disrespectful to their aunt (who had no children of her own). I said to them, "Did you not hear me say her wish was for me to share the love of Jesus and to leave them laughing?" These were the stories we talked about together. It was her desire to help people grieve with laughter. I learned that some people do not think it appropriate to laugh in the dark. They have missed God's song of laughter even in the midst of great pain.

At the funeral of one of my closest friends who had committed suicide leaving behind a wife and two small children, I told a few funny stories about him. Though the seriousness of his death was profound, and many were greatly bereaved, to honor his memory was more than concentrating on how he died and that he was dead, we needed to remember how he lived. Even today, when I think of him, a smile comes to my face while my heart feels like a spear had been stuck in it. To know him was to spend a good deal of time laughing together.

The Song Of Laughter

When I sit down with a family who has had a death, I ask them to tell me about the person: hobbies, places they lived, what made them laugh and cry, what was their passion. I cannot ever remember having a funeral where there wasn't something in it that made us smile or laugh.

While writing this chapter, I received a call that my brother-in-law died suddenly of a heart-attack. All the feelings of numbness, denial and pain took over me. It couldn't be so! I immediately jumped in the car and went to the house to be with the family.

People began arriving. Stories were being told. Many stories were told through tears, yet laughter was being heard. He was a man who loved life and lived it to the fullest. He was an attorney, a basketball referee, a tax preparer, and could do just about anything that needed doing.

The day of his funeral I was to have the eulogy. Following me were four attorney friends of his who would speak. Each had known him for many years. The first one got up and said, "I would not be here today for just anyone because I am 3-hours post-surgery from having a colonoscopy this morning. The congregation erupted in laughter. He went on to tell a couple of hilarious stories and when he sat down the next speaker stood up and said, "I never thought I would hear the word 'colonoscopy' from the pulpit of a church!"

When the service ended, and we were in the reception hall, several came to me and said, "this was a true celebration of life. We loved the stories and the laughter. Sure, we are sad, but we needed to laugh. Thanks."

My father was my mentor, my pastor, my friend, my brother in the ministry, my fishing buddy, my associate pastor, my confidant, and hero. He was a prince of a man and I loved him with my whole heart. He was a true gentleman and yet his very countenance commanded respect. He was a statesman of the church and a pastor par excellence. He always kept himself well-groomed, his fingernails clean, and his shoes polished. He was the "mother hen" of his family and was "true-blue". In all of my life, he is the most forgiving person I have ever known.

At 84 years of age, Dad suffered a stroke. After a week at Emory University Hospital he came home only to have another stroke three weeks later. This time, we had to put him in a nursing facility. His transitioned from a man who took extra good care of himself, to almost baby-like qualities. He suffered the indignity of having to wear adult diapers, he could not brush his own teeth or bathe himself. There would be days his mind was crystal-clear and other days he would accuse those in the room with him of trying to poison him.

There were times with him that what he said was actually funny. I felt horrible suppressing a laugh until talking with a physician friend of mine who said, "That is not making fun of him, it is cherishing him and the silly sweet things he says." It seemed conflicting to me to be grieving over his condition and yet finding humor as well.

One morning he called me and told me I had to come and get him out of "there." He said there were women trying to have sex with him. I asked him why he thought that. He said, "They have tried to take off my clothes." Trying to speak rationally to a person whose mind is jumbled from a stroke is next to impossible. I assured him that I would take care to see that no one was trying to hurt him and that I had personally sent those women to help him bathe and dress. He could trust them. He settled down and allowed them to do their work. After hanging up the phone, I could only imagine the looks on the faces of those nurses thinking my 84-year-old stroke victim father was accusing them of sexual impropriety!

Dad was one who loved to play pranks on people. One time he went out of state to a church convention and came home with a glass he had bought that when it was filled with water and a person put it to their lips, water would dribble down their chin. He would often put it at the guest's place in our home when mother was serving a nice meal. (She was not wild about the joke glass). Dad would anticipate what would happen and get great joy from pulling one on a friend.

He also had a spoon with a fly glued on it. He would set it by the plate of a guest and watch their reaction to see if they would try to wave it away, or simply leave it and not use the spoon.

On the evening of his death, all of the family was gathered around him. He had been in a coma for several days and the end was near. We told stories sang hymns and loved on him. He took a deep breath and exhaled and then did not breathe. My brother turned to us and said, "He's gone." Suddenly, he took another big breath and continued breathing for another few minutes before doing the same thing again. Silence. We waited longer. "Now he is gone." Once again, he began to breathe. My oldest sister leaned over him and said, "Are you playing one of your tricks on us? Is this a prank? You want the last laugh." We all began to laugh because that would be just like him. And then his breathing stopped, and he was truly gone. But he died the way he lived, making us laugh and enjoy life even in the midst of darkness and death.

There have times in my darkest moments where I would remember an experience that brought me laughter and I would laugh until tears streamed down my face. We call that a "bellylaugh" in our home. In the midst of laughter, the light of hope and joy comes, and I know that the darkness will not consume me.

Another of God's songs in the night is the song of laughter.

Songs In The Night

When you walk through a storm
Hold your head up high
And don't be afraid of the dark.
At the end of the storm
Is a golden sky
And the sweet silver song of a lark.

Walk on through the wind,
Walk on through the rain,
Tho' your dreams be tossed and blown.
Walk on, walk on
With hope in your heart
And you'll never walk alone,
You'll never walk alone.*

Come, ye disconsolate, where'er ye languish,
Come to the mercy seat, fervently kneel.
Here bring your wounded hearts, here tell your anguish;
Earth has no sorrow that heav'n cannot heal.

Joy of the desolate, light of the straying,
Hope of the penitent, fadeless and pure!
Here speaks the Comforter, tenderly saying,
"Earth has no sorrow that heav'n cannot cure."

Here see the bread of life, see waters flowing
Forth from the throne of God, pure from above.
Come to the feast of love; come, ever knowing
Earth has no sorrow but heav'n can remove.**

*Rogers, Richard and Oscar Hammerstein, II. You'll Never walk Alone. From *Carousel,* 1945
**Webbe, Samuel. "Come, Ye Disconsolate." 1740-1816. UMH

CHAPTER 7

The Song of Forgiveness

Several years ago, a friend of mine wrote a book on forgiveness. When it was published, she brought it to me to read. It was well written and theologically sound.

Interestingly, I would discover that she was one of the most unforgiving people I have ever known! She refused to forgive her father for the emotional abuse from her childhood. She has never forgiven employers who relieved her of jobs. Her first husband committee adultery and she has said she would never forgive him for it.

One time, I misunderstood something she had said and when I repeated it among several friends with her there, she yelled at me. She repeated what I had said, and then said that I had totally gotten it wrong. I said to her, "I am so sorry, please forgive me." She turned to me and with great anger said, "Forgiveness is a process." She walked away and to this day has never touched base nor forgiven me. That was many years ago!

Before we judge her too harshly, how about you and me? Do we really forgive those who have hurt us, embarrassed us, abused us, fired us, betrayed us? Forgiveness and loving our enemies are two of the most difficult things Jesus has ever asked his followers

Songs In The Night

to do. What do we do in the dark night when something like this happens to us?

I am not accomplished in the art of forgiveness; however, I have had many opportunities to practice it on others and I have been the recipient more times than I would like to admit.

While my father was the pastor of a church in Atlanta, a new parsonage was bought. The one we were living in was across the street from the church on a busy street where there was almost no place to play. The new one was in a beautiful neighborhood where there were lots of children and space to run and play. The front yard was huge and became the meeting place for the kids to gather to ride bicycles, get up a game of baseball, kickball, or other childhood games.

When we moved in, my mother prepared for a church-wide open house for the congregation to see their new home. In those days, churches had a parsonage committee, usually a group of women who would come to the house from time to time to see if it was kept clean, the furniture upkept, and to know what was needed. One of the members of the parsonage committee was an elderly woman of exquisite taste. She was regal, stately and refined. She often came to the house the week before the open house to help decorate. Shortly before the big day, she came to the house with an antique expensive and gorgeous soup tureen for the center piece on the dining room table. Mother was almost breathless when she saw it. We did not have such things in our home.

After she left, mother gathered my two sisters and me in the dining room and showed us the soup tureen. She told us how valuable it was, and we were to stay out of the dining room. It was off limits. Mother kept the doors to the dining room closed so we would not go in. She used the word 'forbidden.'

The big event was scheduled on a mid-Sunday afternoon after worship. The Saturday before, mother left us at home to go shopping for extra "finger-foods" to serve the next day. While she was away, my sister and I got into an argument. She was holding a pencil in

The Song Of Forgiveness

her hand and stabbed my arm with it. I was very angry and began to chase her around the house. While trying to find space to get away from me, she opened the door to the dining room and ran in. I followed close behind her. Her arm bumped the table and the ladle fell off the tureen and fell on the floor and broke. When she stopped, I ran into her and the tureen also came tumbling down, breaking into several pieces. We were mortified! We knew mother would be extremely angry at us because she had banned the room from us.

When she came home, she walked into the dining room and saw the broken tureen. She burst into tears, holding the broken pieces of the tureen in her hands.

She came into our rooms and took us by the hands and together we walked up the street to where the woman lived who let us borrow the tureen. I was shaking as we stood on her front porch waiting for her to open the door. Mother had the broken tureen in a bag. She had told us we were to tell what had happened and to ask forgiveness.

The door opened and we were graciously escorted into the living room. Mother opened the bag and as she pulled out the broken tureen, the tears streamed down her face. She told her that the dining room was off limits and we had disobeyed. My sister and I sheepishly spoke our words of sorrow and hid behind mother's back.

Poised and calm, she spoke to mother first and said, "I had planned all along to give you the tureen after the open house. Please do not be upset that it is broken." She looked at us and said, "I forgive you, but you need to always mind your mother." She hugged us, and with great compassion and love changed the subject and by the end of our time there, we were smiling and knew we would remain alive!!!

That is not the end of the story. Mother went back home, and she and my father glued the broken pieces back together. From the front, it was not too noticeable. She kept it on the dining room table and every dining room table for the rest of her life. It became a symbol for her of grace and forgiveness. She never wanted to forget the sweet, sweet fragrance of mercy, redemption and forgiveness.

Songs In The Night

When mother died, my siblings and I gathered to divide up her things. When the tureen surfaced, we all wanted it. My younger brother was the recipient. It continues to be visible in his home these many years since mother's death. I will always carry the memory with me and be reminded of it when someone hurts me or those I love.

As a pastor, I have been with people who have had horrible pains inflicted upon them: rape, murder, betrayal, abandonment, arson, assault, larceny, burglary, kidnapping, bullying and destruction from alcoholism and drug abuse. Forgive?

In one of my churches, there was a family that was very close-knit. The husband was an architect and the wife a physician (neonatologist). They had four children and one grandchild. They were regularly in worship and involved in the church. Their youngest son played on one of my son's baseball team. We were together at the field, in church and in their home. They were great people of deep faith and worked for the betterment of the community.

One week, the wife had a newborn little boy, born several weeks premature, that had a multitude of health issues. For 48 hours straight she walked the baby, gave it medicine and did all in her power to keep him alive. At his death, two of her nurses accused her of smothering the baby causing his death.

She was arrested, her picture and name on the front page of every major paper in the surrounding area and a trial date set. Her husband lost his job. The attorney's fees were astronomical and soon they lost their house and had to move into a small rented place.

Her trial resulted in a "hung" jury. The district attorney decided not to re-try the case because of a lack of evidence.

What the nurses saw was her hand over the baby's face and assumed she was trying to suffocate the child when in actuality she was trying to hold his tongue down, so he wouldn't swallow it.

She was a loving mother and grandmother. She had spent two whole days without sleep, trying to keep him alive and then falsely accused of murder. She was innocent, but now she had no home, no money, and was ruined as a physician. Her good name had been trampled through the mud.

After the trial, I asked her what she and her family were going to do. She said, "We are moving to Texas to be near our parents and to start all over again. What else can I do? I must learn to trust again, to strive to forgive, and continue to help others." After a brief pause, she said, "My family is looking to me to see how I will handle all of this. It will be the defining part of my life. I've got to do it right! I must forgive. Pray for me."

Can we forgive like that?

During that same year as this physician's trial, another trial was going on at the same time. It was a child-sexual abuse case. The family involved was one of the pillars of the community. The trial split the community into factions. The highlights:

- The parents were dear friends of mine. I was in their home often as a young pastor. The wife taught me how to cook. She and her husband helped furnish my first apartment. They were greatly involved in the church and community. I would have left my children with them to babysit if needed. I thought of them like "second" grandparents.
- Their daughters (two of them) had three daughters ages 7-9. They discovered their daughters had been molested. After the physician's confirmation, their little girls said, "It was grandpa."
- More horrible reports came out about their situation: the grandfather would molest his granddaughters and then send them out to the grandmother for her to clean them up and apply medicine.
- The trial lasted over a month. More atrocious discoveries surfaced. In addition to molestation, there was "devil worship" involved.

Songs In The Night

The trial ended in a mistrial. It was discovered that some $600,000 had been removed from the grandparents account during the trial and it was believed that some of the jury members were paid off to ensure the mistrial. The children said that they would not put their daughters through another trial. It was over. They turned to the grandparents and said "From this moment on, you are dead to us. We never will see you again."

Both daughters would move to other cities. However, several years later, the daughters visited their parents and made peace with them. Forgiveness was offered. The parents did not live much longer as both were up in age by then, but they died forgiven.

I wondered if I had been in their shoes if I could have offered the "olive branch" of reconciliation and forgiveness. Could you?

Corrie Ten Boom was a survivor of the Holocaust. For years she and her sister Betsy were in a concentration camp where they were abused, starved, mocked, and made to work long and hard hours. She was made to strip in front of the officers to be inspected. It was a life of horrible indecency. Her sister would die there. By a clerical error, Corrie was released. She spent her life spreading the love of Christ often preaching in churches around Europe.

One Sunday evening, she preached at church and at the end of her sermon she invited all who would, to come down to the altar and give their lives to Christ. She walked from the pulpit to the front of the church to greet any coming down. To her horror and shock, one of her captors in the concentration camp began walked toward her. She began to panic. He had treated her sub-humanly. He was evil. Could she welcome someone like him? If she didn't, her message of grace and new life was false, indeed a fake.

When he stood in front of her, she held out her hand. He took it and told her he was sorry and wanted to live a new life in Christ. She prayed with him and for him. Then she opened her arms and enfolded him in a holy hug! Both received love and forgiveness.

The Song Of Forgiveness

Corrie lived by her words: "When a train goes through a tunnel and it gets dark, you don't throw away the ticket and jump out. You sit still and trust the engineer." She trusted God to be with her when she reached out and welcomed her former guard into Christ's church.

Perhaps the greatest act of forgiveness was seen when Jesus was nailed to a cross. He looked out on those who were hurting him, those who had betrayed him, and those who left him to die alone, and he uttered aloud "Father forgive them, they know not what they do."

While the disciples were gathered together in fear following the crucifixion, Jesus appears to them. His first words were not "You dirty rats, why did you leave me to die alone?" He didn't say, "You are the worst people in the world." His first words were, "Peace be with you." In fact, he never mentions his crucifixion to them. Instead, he spends time with them and offers them the keys to the kingdom!

Since I don't have the soup tureen, I carry a small cross in my pocket to remind me that I have been forgiven and I need to forgive.

In a cemetery outside of Atlanta is a grave with only one word on it:

Forgiven

We cannot truly live unless we can forgive and accept forgiveness. Let that sink in. To carry around deep anger and bitterness only hurts and destroys the ones carrying it. To be free, really free, forgive.

When the dark night of deepest hurt seems to engulf me, and I want to get revenge on the one who has wounded me, instead of making things worse by fighting pain with inflicting pain, I go back to my childhood and remember the tureen, or look at the cross that hangs on my wall and the sweet, sweet song of forgiveness sweeps over my soul and I know what I must do to be whole again: listen to God's song of forgiveness, and get about making it happen.

The light shines in the darkness
and the darkness does not overcome it.

John 1:5 NRSV

Chapter 8

The Song of a Child

I have heard that people with dementia and/or Alzheimer's disease may not remember what happened to them yesterday or last week or even last year, but they can remember the songs of their childhood. Indeed, it has been noted that some who have almost no memory at all can still sing "Jesus loves me" or pray "now I lay me down to sleep." These are songs and prayers from their childhood.

The great theologian Karl Barth, one who wrote thousands of pages (volumes) of Church Dogmatics, was asked in an interview one day to summarize his life's work. Without hesitation he looked at the reporter and said, "Jesus loves me this I know, for the Bible tells me so."

When the darkness of life settles in on us, seek out a child. Jesus put them on his knee and told his disciples "to such belongs the kingdom of God."

My grandchildren fill my heart with love and humor. If I want to know the truth of something, I will ask them. Children are usually forthcoming and hold nothing back.

A case in point: I was in the car with my 4-year-old granddaughter, Anna. We began singing some songs she had learned in church. My wife was driving, I was on the passenger side and she was in the backseat. As we began singing, she stopped and said, "D-Dad, don't sing. It's bad!" She is right. I can't sing very well, but I love to anyway.

She is the one who sat on Santa's lap at Christmas and when he asked her if she had been a good little girl, she looked up at him and said, "Well actually, my sister and I have had a little trouble!" She is honest to a fault!

She is also my grandchild who suffers from chronic juvenile rheumatoid arthritis. She wears glasses due to uveitis caused from arthritis. There are days she can barely walk because her knee is swollen. At times she will say "I hurt all over." It is amazing to be around her. She does not want to miss anything her big sisters are doing. She never wants to miss "school" or play time. Only occasionally does she complain, and it is simply sharing what hurts.

Unlike her, there are times I am all too willing to voice my aches and pains to someone who will listen. And then I think of Anna. She gets up every morning and strives to do the "normal" routine. She gets excited about going to school, playing outside, and being with friends. Nothing holds her back from giving everyone hugs and kisses.

Children help us to rediscover life. Get on your knees and walk with a child around a room. You will see things differently. Do the same thing outside. The world looks larger.

When my grandchildren come to the house, I am amazed how creative they are. They can take almost anything I would discard and make something useful from it. My wife and I live on Lake Lanier and in autumn when the water goes down a bit, the grandkids like to get plastic garbage bags and go around the lake picking up garbage. It is almost a game for them! One year we gathered eight bags full! What I would consider drudgery, they turned into fun.

The same goes for setting the table, helping my wife cook, making cards for loved ones who are sick, and at Christmas, making all their gifts to give the family. It seems they never tire from all they are doing. In short, they live life to the fullest.

The Song Of A Child

On some days when the darkness has surrounded me and all I want to do is go to bed and pull the covers over my head, I quiet myself and listen. Often, I hear the sounds of the children laughing over "slobbers on their stomachs" or singing crazy songs or hear their dialogue as they play "house'" When I remember their sweet hugs and excitement about coming to our house for the weekend, I feel overjoyed. I even begin to smile. The world looks brighter, full of hope, and I don't want to miss out on a minute of each day.

Many years ago, our family was gathered for Christmas morning opening of gifts. All had been opened and I got up to help my wife cook breakfast. She said to me, "Sit down. There is one more gift." And to my utter astonishment, a little brown chocolate lab puppy came running around the corner into the living room straight into my arms. She could not stop wiggling with excitement and licking my face. Then she wanted to jump down and explore every inch of the house. She pointed out things to me that I had not seen in years.

When I would take her outside, she would take a few steps and then lift her nose to smell the air. She smelled in all directions. Her ears perked up and she would listen. Finally, she would stretch her legs and go after something she had seen or smelled. Each day, she had the same routine.

She has helped me to slow down and "smell the roses" of life. I pay more attention to what surrounds me. I look for the small lessons in life. She has taught me to appreciate things I took for granted.

Her name is Belle. She is a "child" to me. She is smart. She knows exactly where I keep her treats, her leash, and food. She knows not to get up on the sofa unless I give the command. What is uncanny is how she remembers the exact hour each day we usually take a walk around the neighborhood. She will sit and look at me and in her high voice make a couple of yips. It is time to go outside.

Where I live there are lots of woods and water. We see many deer, rabbits, squirrels, turkeys, (sometimes a snake or two), woodchucks, Canadian geese, ducks, and multitudes of birds. Occasionally a fish

Songs In The Night

will jump out of the water. I call my wife, or she calls me, and we go to the glass porch and look out and watch the wildlife. They do not carry around grudges. They do not worry about tomorrow. They live for today. They inspire me to do the same.

It is the songs of children and the creatures of the earth that help me move from darkness to light. Do you know these songs:

> All things bright and beautiful,
> All creatures great and small,
> All things wise and wonderful:
> The Lord God made them all.
>
> Each little flow'r that opens,
> Each little bird that sings,
> He made their glowing colors,
> He made their tiny wings.
>
> The purple-headed mountains,
> The river running by,
> The sunset and the morning
> That brightens up the sky.
>
> The cold wind in the winter,
> The pleasant summer sun,
> The ripe fruits in the garden,
> He made them everyone.
>
> The tall trees in the greenwood,
> The meadows where we play,
> The rushes by the water,
> To gather every day.
>
> He gave us eyes to see them,
> And lips that we might tell

The Song Of A Child

How great is God Almighty,
Who has made all things well.*

And then there is the old familiar one that reminds us of the greatness of God.

He's got the whole world in His hands,
He's got the whole world in His hands,
He's got the whole world in His hands,
He's got the whole world in His hands.

He's got my brothers and my sisters in His hands,
He's got my brothers and my sisters in His hands,
He's got my brothers and my sisters in His hands,
He's got the whole world in His hands.

He's got the sun and the rain in His hands,
He's got the moon and the stars in His hands,
He's got the wind and the clouds in His hands,
He's got the whole world in His hands.

He's got the birds and the bees, in His Hands
He's got the birds and the bees, in His hands
He's got the beast of the field in His hands
He's got the whole world in His hands.

He's got the rivers and the mountains in His hands,
He's got the oceans and the seas in His hands,
He's got you and he's got me in His hands,
He's got the whole world in His hands.

---

* Monk, Edwin George, George Mcbeth Mcphee, Cecil Francis Alexander. "All things Bright and Beautiful". Palace Music Co./Shawnee Press, Inc.

Songs In The Night

>He's got everybody here in His hands,
>He's got everybody there in His hands,
>He's got everybody everywhere in His hands,
>He's got the whole world in His hands.*

God will give songs in the night and one of the stanzas is the song of "all creatures great and small."

---

*American Spiritual. 1927. (first recorded By Laurie London) UMH

When the storms of life are raging stand by me
When the storms of life are raging stand by me
When the world is tossing me like a ship upon the sea
Thou who rulest wind and water stand by me

When the midst of tribulation stand by me
when the midst of tribulation stand by me
When the hosts of hell assail and my strength begins to fail
Thou who never lost a battle stand by me

When the midst of faults and failures stand by me
When the midst of faults and failures stand by me
When I do the best I can and my friends misunderstand
Thou who knowest all about me stand by me

When I'm growing old and feeble stand by me
When I'm growing old and feeble stand by me
When my life becomes a burden and
I'm nearing chilly Jordan
O Thou Lily of the Valley stand by me (stand by me)*

*Tindley, Charles Albert. "When the Storms of Life are Raging." Ca 1906. UMH

CHAPTER 9

The Song of Hope

The television is off but the scenes from it still play over and over in my mind. Tonight, it is a scene from Las Vegas where a man has skillfully and strategically planned the killing of innocent people gathered to hear an outdoor concert. In all, fifty-nine are killed. Many are injured. Chaos is everywhere. New heroes are made. Fear is rampant.

December 14, 2012, in Newtown, Connecticut, twenty-year-old Adam Lanza fatally shot twenty children between six and seven years old, as well as six adult staff members at Sandy Hook Elementary School. Prior to driving to the school, he shot and killed his mother at their Newtown home. In a matter of seconds, the sound of parents crying over their losses would be heard all over the world. The sounds keep penetrating my mind as I lie in the dark trying to be at ease after a profoundly sad day.

Hurricanes, tornadoes, tsunamis, earthquakes, terrorism, disease, poverty, injustice, school shootings, human trafficking, drug lords, and cyber-attacks are but some of the "tigers" in our darkness. Add to those, marital strain, the stress of parenting, betrayal of a friend, being passed over for a raise, and the news of a loved one who is dying or has died.

My father had an aunt who lived alone in a small rural home. He would take me with him to visit her as often as he could because she was one of his favorite relatives. She would open the door and give him a big hug and kiss on the cheek and invite us in. No sooner than we had sat down she would say, "I hope I don't fall asleep while we are talking. I just can't sleep any more. Too many things crawl out at me in the night." As I have aged, I understand what she means. Oh, I can get to sleep, but I don't always stay that way. I can wake in the wee hours of the morning with "things crawling" out of my mind. Usually most of these "crawling" things, thank God, never come to reality.

However, for many of our fore-parents, their worst dreams were realized. Amazingly, hope was never destroyed. Their stories inspire and point us to hope.

In 1994 Murry Sidlin, was walking down Minneapolis's Hennepin Avenue past the Bryn Mawr Bookstore when an outdoor display of $3 books caught his eye. One was Joza Kara's *Music in Terezin, 1941-1945,* a primer about the musical life in the military fortress north of Prague that the Nazis turned into a concentration camp. One of its two-page stories concerned a Jewish conductor and pianist named Rafael Schachter, who during his three years at the camp organized a volunteer choir of 150 prisoners and taught them to perform Giuseppe Verdi's choral *Requiem* by memory sixteen times. He bought the book and what he read boggled his mind: sixteen performances in a concentration camp! Why would a Jewish conductor turn to a choral requiem of a Catholic mass in the face of the Nazi Final Solution? He learned Schachter was deported to Auschwitz and then sent to three other camps before dying on a death march about a month prior to Czech liberation in April 1945.

June 23, 1944, SS officers escorted an International Red Cross team inspecting Terezin. In the weeks prior to the visit, the Nazis had forced the inmates to make the camp look upbeat and happy. Flowers and gardens were planted. A playground was built for children. A soccer match was staged. Parks that Jews were not allowed to use were beautified. The last six hours, Schachter was ordered to assemble his choir and perform for them. SS officers and other Nazi handlers were in the audience. In the face of this choreographed lie, Schachter and his choir were going to stand up and sing an act of defiance in the face of their oppressors. It was called by the prisoners The Defiant Requiem. This was, after all, a place where people were murdered, where one group of supposedly cultured and civilized human beings decided to annihilate another.

The response of the prisoners was: 2400 lectures, sixteen performances of the Verdi Requiem, 38 performances of *The Bartered Bride*, 50 performance of the children's opera *Brundibar*, and performances of Mendelsohns *Elijah*, Puccini's opera *Tosca*, and Mozart's *The Magic Flute*.

It was vitally important for the Jewish prisoners to say to the Red Cross representatives and the Nazis gathered there through their music, **"You may be our captors, but we are free."** We are energized, valued human beings who choose to respond with the best of humankind.

The *Verdi Requiem*, next to Handel's *Messiah* must be the most performed oratorio in the world. The Catholics borrowed the Songs of David to construct the mass, so these people were borrowing back the mass. Imagine Verdi knowing how his music was used, he would be on his knees with tears to know that those people, oppressed as they were, reached out for his music.*

I cannot see myself in an arena facing hungry lions who will destroy me, but many of our fore-parents did just that. For their faith, they were fed to the lions.

I cannot imagine being lifted onto a stake of wood and set on fire because I professed Jesus as Lord, but many of our fore-parents did just that.

(John Hopkins Magazine p29-34 "May it Go to the Heart" by Bret McCabe. Volume 64 No. 4 Winter 2012)

I cannot imagine being put on a train stuffed beyond capacity with other people and being taken to the coldest part of the world and forced into brutal labor and then, being taken to the gas chambers and put to death. But many of our fore-parents suffered in this way.

I cannot imagine having to watch as my spouse, children and parents are put to death in front of me, then I am stripped of my clothes, starved and abused, but many of our fore-parents did. They were killed for their faith.

In Elie Wiesel's *Night*, Eliezer is a Jewish teenager, a devoted student of the Talmud from Sighet, in Hungarian Transylvania. In the spring of 1944, the Nazis occupy Hungary. A series of increasingly repressive measures are passed, and the Jews of Eliezer's town are forced into small ghettos within Sighet. Before long, they are rounded up and shipped out to the death camps of Burkenau, and Auschwitz. Throughout this slim narrative, Eliezer reflects on the nature of God in response to the atrocities he witnesses. In one pivotal scene, he describes the execution of three Jews, among whom is a young child.

One day, as we returned from work, we saw three gallows, three black ravens, erected on the Appelplatz. *Roll call. The* SS *surrounding us, machine guns aimed at us: the usual ritual. Three prisoners in chains – and, among them, the little* pipel, *the sad-eyed angel.*

The SS *seemed more preoccupied, more worried, than usual. To hang a child in front of thousands of onlookers was not a small matter. The head of the camp read the verdict. All eyes were on the child. He was pale, almost calm, but he was biting his lips as he stood in the shadow of the gallows.*

This time, the Lagerkapo *refused to act as executioner. Three* SS *took his place.*

The Song Of Hope

The three condemned prisoners together stepped onto the chairs. In unison, the nooses were placed around their necks.

"Long live liberty!" shouted the two men.

But the boy was silent.

"Where is merciful God, where is He?" someone behind me was asking.

At the signal, the three chairs were tipped over.

Total silence in the camp. On the horizon, the sun was setting.

"Caps off!" screamed the Lageralteste. *His voice quivered. As for the rest of us, we were weeping.*

"Cover your heads!"

Then came the march past the victims. The two men were no longer alive. Their tongues were hanging out, swollen and bluish. But the third rope was still moving: the child, too light, was still breathing…

And so, he remained for more than half an hour, lingering between life and death, writhing before our eyes. And we were forced to look at him at close range. He was still alive when I passed him. His tongue was still red, his eyes not yet extinguished.

Behind me, I heard the same man asking:

"For God's sake, where is God?"

And from within me, I heard a voice answer:

"Where is He? This is where – hanging here from this gallows…"

The young child seems to be a "Christ" figure and we hear the echoes of Him who said, "my God, my God, why have you forsaken me."*

---

*Wiesel, Elise. Night. New York: Hill & Wang. 1960

It seems there is no hope. The Spirit of God has died with the little one. But that is not the whole story. Even Wiesel doesn't end the story there. *Night* is only the first of a trilogy and, while Wiesel's characters wrestle in their relationship to God, God is very much alive.

Where is God? Where is God visible?

*……in the workers who responded on September 11, 2001, striving to rescue people from the burning buildings, through the American Red Cross,

*……in the churches bringing needed relief,

*……in the American public digging deep in their pockets to help the families who lost loved ones;

*……in the Amish community going to the home of the family whose husband/father murdered several of their own children bringing them food and forgiveness.

*…….in Pope John Paul II going to the prison and visiting his would-be assassin and blessing him, forgiving him and offering him friendship.

*…...when we come together for the greater good of the world

God is moving within and among us today, leading us through the darkness of death into the joy of abundant life and giving us the gift of hope.

The Song Of Hope

How firm a foundation, ye saints of the Lord,
Is laid for your faith in His excellent word!
What more can He say than to you He hath said—
To you who for refuge to Jesus have fled?

"Fear not, I am with thee, oh, be not dismayed,
For I am thy God, and will still give thee aid;
I'll strengthen thee, help thee, and cause thee to stand,
Upheld by My gracious, omnipotent hand.

"When through the deep waters I call thee to go,
The rivers of sorrow shall not overflow;
For I will be with thee thy trouble to bless,
And sanctify to thee thy deepest distress.

"When through fiery trials thy pathway shall lie,
My grace, all-sufficient, shall be thy supply;
The flame shall not harm thee; I only design
Thy dross to consume and thy gold to refine.

"The soul that on Jesus doth lean for repose,
I will not, I will not, desert to his foes;
That soul, though all hell should endeavor to shake,
I'll never, no never, no never forsake."*

*Anonymous

Chapter 10

The Song of Love

Twenty years of marriage, two beautiful children, a host of friends, a cozy house and two dogs set the scene of dear friends. Friday afternoon, his car came into the driveway and he bounded up the steps into the house. He said to his wife, "Let's go get an ice cream before the kids get home from school." Without purse, make-up or changing clothes, she hopped in the car anticipating a quick date with the love of her life.

After bringing the banana-split to the table, he took her hands in his and said, "we need to talk. I love you as a person, but I am not in love with you anymore. I want us to divorce." She sat in silence. Numb. Scared. Overwhelmed. It couldn't be. Twenty years! How? Why? What happened? She said, "take me home." On the way, he began to pour out that he had fallen in love with his administrative assistant. They were each going to divorce their spouses and get married. He had it all planned. He showed her what was needed to do to the house to get it ready to be put up for sale. He showed her the apartment he had picked out, and then produced their banking information and how much she would get.

She tip-toed into the bathroom and called me. Through her tears she said, "you know what? I still love him. Can you believe that? I still love him."

Several years later at the graduation of one of her children, she said to me, "I will always love him." She admits that she would never take him back as a husband (and he tried to go back to her after his second divorce). She never hated him. She did not try to make the divorce difficult. She took the higher road and has modeled for her children and all who know her, the depth of genuine love.

When my oldest son was in the fourth grade, his baseball team had their end of the year celebration on a huge farm in rural Fayette County. The place was beautiful: acres of green fields, a small pond, a place with picnic tables and space for the kids to run and play. A path led from the picnic area to the house where there was a swimming pool.

We feasted on hotdogs, potato chips and colas. Our conversation was about the teams wins and losses until it was time to go to the swimming pool for fun games and the awarding of trophies.

Several of the team members walked with me up the hill toward the house. The whole pasture area was protected by barbed-wire and the gate where we had to pass through, was also one of barbed-wire. Since I was the first adult to get to the gate, I lifted the lock off the post, and the heavy weight of barbed wire came down on me. It ripped into my stomach. I would not let go because I didn't want any of the children to be hurt. I gently walked back and opened the gate wider, so the kids could run through. My wife was not far behind and when she got to me, she helped me lift the weight off of me. My shirt was torn, and I was bleeding.

I told her that I was hurt but did not want anyone to know it. I could make it to my car and drive to the hospital. As I fled down the road, I thought of how Jesus suffered for others. I felt a warm glow coming over me as I pondered that my taking the suffering, so the kids would not be hurt was just like Jesus. I was proud of myself.

Upon arriving at the hospital, I was immediately taken to a room where my wounds were cleaned and stitched. Then I heard a lot of noise coming from the entrance to the emergency room. A young boy was coming in. His father had hit him in the head with a golf club as a means of punishment. As they rolled him past my door, I caught a glimpse of him. His head was a mass of blood, knots and bruising.

The father was arrested. The boy died from his wounds.

As I witnessed the police arresting the father, the silence from the little boy, I felt a great sense of failure. Would I have held the barbed-wire fence for a man who would abuse his child like this one? Suddenly, I realized I had a lot more to learn. I would need to grow a bigger heart. I was not close to being as Jesus in His ability to love.

How did Jesus do it? From the cross, his hands and feet bleeding from nails hammered into them, the lack of support for his body that would eventually cause him to suffocate, and soldiers mocking him, he would say "Father, forgive them. They know not what they do." Every time I think of it, I am amazed at his response. Can we love like that?

I had a professor in college who worked for over twenty years on a definition of love. Dr. Robert Preston Price finally arrived at this:

"Love is the wishing and wanting the highest and best for others, being willing aggressively to work for it, and if need be, to die for it."

I think it is a great start, but I would add the following to it;

Love is the wishing and wanting the highest and best for others, being willing aggressively to work for it, and if need be, to die for it, *and expecting nothing in return.* If we do things for others with the intention of getting something back can it really be love? Naturally, we all want to be loved. It has been proven that a newborn cannot live without human touch and loving. However, authentic love is giving without thought of return.

A parent dishes out love on their baby and the baby cannot articulate love back. When a couple marries, the pastor asks: "Will you love him/her in sickness and health, for better or worse?" The pastor does not say, "Are you 'in love' or "Will you love as long as you feel like it?" Rather, "Will you choose to love even if the spouse can't return it?"

I had a man in one of my former churches who married the love of his life. On their honeymoon she suffered a stroke (age 22) and was totally immobile, unable to speak, and bedridden for ten years until her death. He took care of her every need. He stood by her, loved on her, and gave her his best.

Parents must teach their children how to love in word and action. For the first few years of life, children are, for the most part, self-consumed. They have difficulty sharing. They want everything for themselves. They always want to win. But that is not the healthy way to life (and yet many adults still act that way!!!). In learning to share their things, they are implementing love. In graciously losing, they are loving. In giving, without expecting in return, they are learning the real meaning of love.

Children will begin to understand as they watch the parent sacrifice for their family. My own parents did without so that my siblings and I could have what we needed and some of what we wanted. My mother rarely went to the beauty parlor. Dad loved golf, but seldom played. Instead, the money they would have spent on themselves was used to provide us piano lessons, horse-back riding lessons, scouts, and camps.

Mom was one who could make a dollar last a week! She saved S &H Green Stamps from the grocery store and after filling several books would turn them in and get a piece of equipment for the kitchen to help her with cooking for the family. She sewed a lot of our clothes. We would go to the store and get new clothes for Easter, but usually she made her own dress.

The Song Of Love

Throughout my life, I witnessed my parents using the best of stewardship to help the family, but also to help others. Even when money was at its tightest, they tithed (giving the first 10% of their income to the church). They gave my sisters, brother and me envelopes from the church (52 in all) so we could take our offering each week. We did not leave home for church without it!

Though my father was not one who said "I love you" very often, he showed love 24/7/365! He was not raised where such words were spoken often so that when they were, they were meaningful. They were not syrupy, sentimental cotton candy words. They had great depth and power.

I grew up in a home where my parents read the Bible daily, we had prayer at each meal and at bedtime, and we were expected to help others. My parents were strict and expected us to do our best. Their agendas did not center on our schedules, but theirs which was always for the betterment of the family. If vacation was planned and I had a baseball tournament, we went on vacation. Our individual events were important but the whole family experience took precedence. We were far from being a perfect family, but love permeated the house. We knew without question that we were loved.

Far too many today are raised in homes where parents will shower their children with everything they want, but are rarely home. It seems that they are mostly involved in their activities to ensure that they are on the best teams and have the best coaches, so that their children will be pro one day! Kids receive trophies for everything they do, just for participating. The home life centers around the children, and not the whole family.

When my oldest son was playing baseball in elementary school, one of the parents shouted out to their son who was up to bat, "If you don't get on base, don't come home." Surprisingly, it was the mother shouting in hateful anger.

I witnessed not only parents, but grandparents shouting horrible things at their own as well as players from the other team. These were elementary age children. It was horrifying.

We need to teach our children that it is ok to lose. It is ok to come in second. Our children need to know that our love is not dependent on what they do, but who they are.

Love is strong. The author of the Song of Solomon (8:6-7) says "love is strong as death." Love is more powerful than evil. Love is the greatest force in the world.

One of my closest friends was diagnosed with malignant melanoma of the eye. He went to the finest eye doctors in the country and they performed a surgery on him where they could shrink the tumor. After a week of intensive chemotherapy, the tumor was gone. He flew back home, and we rejoiced and celebrated that his cancer was gone.

He went back to work and continued to enjoy life to the fullest. From time-to-time he would call me and say, "have you looked out the window today or gone outside and looked up at the heavens? It is a beautiful day!" Or he would call me and say, "Just wanted to tell you how much you mean to me."

The physicians told him he would have to have a body scan every six months to ensure a melanoma cell didn't travel through his body and attach itself to a vital organ. He did this religiously and every scan showed he was cancer free. He continued to work, to golf, to coach his children in their sports and to be a leader in the church where I was the pastor.

Three years sailed by and he had his body scan the week after Christmas. All was well as usual. However, in January he began to suffer abdominal pains. He didn't think much of it until they became more acute. His physician felt he needed a cat scan. So, the first week of February, he had the scan.

We were to eat lunch on Tuesday afternoon that week. He called me early that morning and told me he would have to take a raincheck for lunch, but could he come to my office right then? I said, "By all means! I am here." He lived near the church and was there in a just a few minutes. I saw him get out of the car and I knew immediately that something was wrong.

He walked in the door and we walked straight into my office and closed the door. I said, 'I can tell something is wrong. What is going on?" He was quiet for a minute and then he asked me about my mother who was in hospice. We talked about her and her condition.

I turned to him and said, "That is not why you are here. What is going on?" He closed his eyes and held out his hand for me to take it. I put my hand in his and he began to pray. I will never forget his words:

"O God, I pray that what I am about tell my friend Dee will not burden him in any way. Pour out your blessings upon him and give him strength as he ministers to this congregation. Bless his mother. Thank you for our friendship. Amen."

I felt scared and nervous. What was going on? He opened his eyes and told me that he had experienced abdominal pains, went to have an MRI and the results were cancer of the liver. The physicians told him he had between 8-10 weeks to live. There was nothing medical science could do for him.

As stunned as I was by his diagnosis, I was even more stunned that in his darkest hour he prayed for me!!! He did not pray for himself, but for the church, my mother and me! His love for us outweighed his own issues of facing death. I would never forget this selfless act of love. It paralleled that of Jesus on the cross praying for the world.

Love is stronger than death.

The cross reminds us of such love, a love so strong that death could not extinguish it. That love is loose in the world today. It is God's eternal song of our value to God. Nothing, nothing will ever be stronger. Nothing will ever change God's love for us. <u>You can count on it.</u>

Isaiah 40

When you pass through the waters, I will be with you
And the waves, will not overcome you
Do not fear, for I have redeemed you
I have called you by name, you are Mine

For I am the Lord your God
I am the Lord your God
(I am) the Holy One of Israel, your Savior

I am the Lord
Do not fear

When you pass through the fire, you'll not be hurt
And the flames will not consume you
Do not fear, for I have redeemed you
I have called you by name, you are Mine

You are the Lord
I'll not fear

You are the Lord*

---

*Hillside United. "When you Pass through the Waters".

Chapter 11

The Song of Light

My oldest sister is a phenomenal instrumentalist. I always loved to listen to her practice the piano in the living room of our home. She can play anything put in front of her from Mozart, to Bach to the latest contemporary songs. She also has a beautiful soprano voice and sometimes she would sing as she played. One of my favorites was the hymn "I Believe". Its words are beautiful and powerful:

> **I believe for every drop of rain that falls**
> **A flower grows**
> **I believe that somewhere in the darkest night**
> **A candle glows**
> **I believe for everyone that goes astray**
> **Someone will come to show the way**
> **I believe**
> **I believe**
>
> **I believe above the storm the smallest prayer**
> **Will still be heard**
> **I believe that someone in the great somewhere**

**Hears every word
Every time I hear a newborn baby cry
Or touch a leaf
Or see the sky
Then I know why
I believe****

The words, "somewhere in the darkest night a candle glows" has always brought me great comfort. A candle in a dark room gives off a soothing glow. I enjoy having candles lit on our dining room table when we eat. We have several candles on the mantel over our fireplace in the den. In winter months we will build a fire and light those candles, turn off all the other lights and sit and watch the flames dancing before us. I can feel stress leaving my shoulders and neck. I begin to relax and breathe deeply. Such light is restorative to my soul.

I have visited in hospitals where newborns are put in "beds" with heat lamps on them. The light brings healing to their health.

It is tradition in the United Methodist Church for two acolytes to process up the aisle of the church each Sunday bringing in light to the two candles on the altar table. Those candles represent the humanity and divinity of Jesus Christ. There is great symbolism as the light enters and leaves the sanctuary. Coming in, the light symbolizes the light of Christ coming into the holy of holies. At the end of the service the light symbolizes the light of Christ's love going out into the world and we are to follow the light out the door and into the world to be light to others.

*Hemphill, Jacob and **David Bell. : Sony/ATV Music Publishing LLC, Universal Music Publishing Group, Kobalt Music Publishing Ltd.**

The Song Of Light

Christmas Eve is often called "The Service of Candles." In our tradition, every person who enters the sanctuary is given a candle to hold through the service until the end when the pastor lights the Christ candle and walks down the aisle lighting candles of the parishioners. When all the candles are lit, the sanctuary lights are turned off and the only light comes from the candles. We sing *Silent Night, Holy Night* as we hold our hands out so the light can be given to us and we pass it to others. It is a moment that quiets our souls in the hustle and bustle of all the Christmas activities of the day.

To those who have lost a loved one, or moved to a new city, or experienced pain in some way, the light of the candles seems to offer hope in the darkness. Then the pastor says, "Behold I bring you good news of great joy, for unto us is born this day a savior, Christ the Lord." Christ was born in the darkness of life. And then the congregation holds up the candles above their heads and sings *Joy to the world the Lord is Come*. On the last stanza, the lights come on, the candles are extinguished, and the acolytes carry out the light for us to follow.

In almost all of the books I have on churches from all over the world, there will be a picture of Christmas Eve candle lighting. Beyond the beauty of the light from the candles, are the faces of those who hold them. They are the faces of peace, hope and expectation.

Next to Easter Sunday, Christmas Eve is the most attended service during the year. Why? We need the light. We need it because humanity has an abundance of darkness.

Interestingly, following Christmas comes the winter months. Medical science has added a new term for those who live where there is little sunlight; Seasonal Affected Disorder or SAD. It is imperative that we have light. Light gives us vitamin D which essential for our skin and our bodies to absorb calcium and promote bone growth as well as other functions.

The highest suicide rate is during these winter months. There is less light and often the worst weather. In some areas of the world, there is only a few hours of sunlight for several months of the year.

Songs In The Night

My wife and I have friends who live in Alaska and they are intentional about getting outside in the few hours of sunlight even if the weather is below zero. They keep their home well lit, so they and their children do not suffer from SAD.

I have always felt it crucial for the church to sing as many songs about "light" as possible not only during the winter months, but all year long. One of them is:

I want to walk as a child of the Light

"I want to walk as a child of the light
I want to follow Jesus
God set the stars to give light to the world
The star of my life is Jesus.

In Him there is no darkness at all
The night and the day are both alike
The Lamb is the light of the city of God
Shine in my heart, Lord Jesus."*

Another: **Jesus, the Light of the world.**

We'll walk in the light, beautiful light,
Come where the dewdrops of mercy shine bright,
Shine all around us by day and by night,
Jesus, the Light of the world.**

Without doubt, my favorite Christmas hymn is *O Holy Night*. It doesn't feel like Christmas without it. Its very words are light in my soul.

---

*Thomerson, Kathleen. "I Want to Walk as a Child of the Light" 1966. UMH
** Bible, Ken. LNWhymns 1998.

The Song Of Light

O Holy Night! The stars are brightly shining,
It is the night of the dear savior's birth.
Long lay the world in sin and error pining, till he
Appeared and the Sprit felt its worth.
A thrill of hope the weary world rejoices,
For yonder breaks a new a new and glorious morn.
Fall on your knees! Oh, hear the angel voices!
O night divine, the night when Christ was born;
O night, O Holy night, O night divine!

Led by the light of faith serenely beaming,
With glowing hearts by His cradle, we stand.
O'er the world a star is sweetly gleaming,
Now come the wisemen from out of the Orient land.
The King of Kings lay thus lowly manger;
In all our trials born to be our friends.
He knows our need, our weakness is no stranger,
Behold your King! Before him lowly bend!

Truly he taught us to love one another,
His law is love and His gospel is peace.
Chains shall he break, for the slave is our brother.
And in His name all oppression shall cease.
Sweet hymns of joy in grateful chorus raise we,
With all our hearts we praise His Holy name
Christ is the Lord! Then ever, ever praise we,
His power and glory ever more proclaim!
His power and glory ever more proclaim!**

*Elderkin, George and Charles Wesley and Jan McNair.
** Cappeau, Placide (words) Adolphe Adam (music). O Holy Night. 1847

Songs In The Night

One Christmas Eve in my time as a pastor, the midnight service was packed to capacity, the singing was awesome, the soloist beautifully sang "O Holy Night" and the service of the candles was wonderful beyond words. The benediction was spoken, the parishioners left to go home, the lights were turned out, the doors locked, and I drove home thinking of getting a good night's sleep and watching the faces of my little children wake up on Christmas morning with excitement and cheer as they saw presents under the tree.

I pulled into the garage and walked into our den. No sooner than I had taken off my coat and sat down on the sofa to rest for a minute the phone rang. One of our couples had been in an accident on the way home from church. They were being rushed to the hospital. I prepared to get back out when the phone rang again. Another couple had been in a car wreck about 30 miles away (they were leaving their parent's home to get back to their own place). Before I left the house, three more calls came in. That was a total of five families in accidents in five different places, in five different hospitals! I would be up all night!!!

Fortunately, only three families were kept overnight, but the other two were badly hurt. I came home in the wee hours of Christmas morning, tired and sad. But those feelings left quickly when the children jumped out of bed and ran into the den. There was a lot of laughing and screams of excitement, hugging and "I love yous" spoken. And then the phone rang again.

The call was from a neighbor of one of our members telling me that there had been an accident this morning. A couple in the church who only had one child, a son who was age twenty, had sent him on ahead of them to the grandparent's home with food for the brunch that was to take place later that morning. As he was making a turn, a truck ran a stop sign and hit him. He was killed instantly.

I told my wife that this was the Christmas from hell! Six accidents had happened in less than twenty-four hours, all with people in my parish! And now, a young man was dead.....on Christmas morning!

The Song Of Light

In addition to finding out that their son had died, the father had lost his job the week before Christmas from a company downsizing employees. He was dealing with depression already.

After being with the family and meeting them at the funeral home, I went home to prepare for the eulogy I would give two days later. I felt angry, I felt sad, I felt that this was the worst thing that could ever happen to parents. What would I say? It was Christmas. Christmas was about light and life and gifts and singing and cheers.

I put away my paper and pen and went into the den to play with the children. By now, it was mid-afternoon. They were tired, and I was tired. We had an early supper, bathed the kids and put them to bed. I turned out all the lights in the front of the house and as I walked back into the den, the only lights shining were those on the Christmas tree. Instead of making my way to bed, I sat down on the sofa and simply gazed at the tree.

The various colors of lighting seemed to represent my multitudes of feelings. Red, blue, yellow, white and green lights blinked at me. As I sat there taking in the kaleidoscope of beauty, it hit me. The name of the newborn child of Bethlehem was Emmanuel which means "God is with us." And God is with us in our anger, our grief, our depression, our laughter, our joy, and our all. That is what I would say in this young man's eulogy. Not only would we remember all the great things about him, but I would focus on Christmas being a time for them to remember, not just the death of their son, but the birth, life and death of one who triumphed over death and is with us in everything we go through in life. I would share about the lights on the Christmas tree. One tree contained all those colors. God's love can enfold all of our feelings and bring beauty from them. Had it not been for the darkness, I would not have noticed, really noticed the lights on the tree. No one wants darkness in their lives, but when it comes, look for the light. It may be just a speck, it may come in various colors, but it will come, bringing assurance that God is with us and the light of God's love will give us eternal life and light.

One of God's songs is the song of light, the kind of light that brings life. Thanks be to God!

CHAPTER 12

The Song of Joy

Over the years of my life, I have learned that everyone handles crisis, tragedy and death differently. Elisabeth Kubler Ross wrote a ground-breaking book many years ago entitled <u>On Death and Dying.</u>* In this great work, she suggests that when a person is told they are dying, or a person is told a loved one is dying they can go through five stages: denial, bargaining, anger, depression, and acceptance. She suggests they do not necessarily come in this order and some people can become stuck in one of these.

Many years ago, the bishop of Georgia and his wife suffered a great loss. Their grandson who worked at an airport in middle Georgia, was decapitated while he was doing his job on the runway as one who directed planes to take off. He was in his early twenties.

The bishop officiated at the funeral. The bishop's wife left the cemetery and did not come out of her house for over a year. She had gone through denial, bargaining and anger but she was stuck in depression.

When we went to visit the bishop and his wife, she was gracious as always. She talked about her grandson, her faith, and her future. The "joy" of God's love was deep inside of her and though she was unable to be out in public, she continued to grow in her devotional life and love for God and others. In short, when she attempted to go to church or even the grocery store, her tears would flow to the point she couldn't drive or complete the smallest task. She said to us, "I just can't accept his death yet. I hope I can, but right now, I am not there."

After a year, the tears began to flow less and less. Her heart would always grieve the short life of her grandson, but it was time for her to step back out into life outside of the house. She would go on to lead retreats and workshops on faith development and Christian missions. She had accepted the death, but she learned as many have, that acceptance does not mean a pain-free life. Acceptance allows us to move on even as we carry the pain of loss.

In one church where I was pastor, a couple had three daughters. One afternoon, the three girls were riding together in their parent's car heading to their grandparent's home. A big truck ran a red light and hit the car on the side of it. The sister sitting on that side of the car was killed instantly. The other two were not hurt at all.

The parents were deeply crushed. The loss of a child is overwhelming. The funeral was attended by the masses. The next Sunday, the parents and their two daughters were in worship as they normally were. Sunday after Sunday they were right there. One day, I went to their home and after visiting for a time, I asked them "How do you do it? You are still in church. You continue to go on in ways that inspire me, yet I can't quite comprehend this." The wife looked at me and said, "God didn't do this to our daughter. We are not angry with God. We are very angry at the truck driver. He was the one responsible for our daughter's death. It will take us a lifetime to work through his negligence, but we will never lose the joy of loving God, others and even this truck driver."

---

*Ross, Elizabeth Kubler. On Death and Dying. MacMillan Company, New York. 1969

The Song Of Joy

Wow! I did not realize one could have joy even in the midst of deep grief, hurt and anger.

I saw this in a father who lost his son on Maundy Thursday. The son committed suicide. Three days later, Easter Sunday, it was tradition at the ending of the service for the choir to sing "Hallelujah" from Handel's *Messiah*. Anyone in the congregation could walk up and sing with the choir. As people began to walk up the steps to the choir loft to join the chancel choir, I saw the father of this young man get up out of the back row and walk down. He went to the men's section and took his place. I watched with anticipation as the music began and he started to sing. He sang out with deep conviction the beautiful words of that chorus. His life was imbedded in the "hallelujah". In his greatest pain, his joy of the love of Jesus Christ was evident.

There are those who have remained with joy in even the worst of times. There are those who lose their joy when the darkness surrounds them. The Bible amazingly shares the raw stories of those who have sinned against God and yet received forgiveness and the restoration of joy to their very souls.

The psalmist says, 'restore unto me the joy of Your salvation." When we look closer at Psalm 51, we know it is a prayer of confession and deep sorrow. The Psalmist is in the dark from his own sins. He pleads for new life, forgiveness and purity of heart. David who had once sung songs of praise to God had committed adultery. He had the woman's husband killed in battle, so he could cover up his sin. However, he was unable to live with his conscience. The newborn son died. David was miserable. Here is what he wrote:

> Have mercy on me, O God,
> according to your steadfast love;
> according to your abundant mercy
> blot out my transgressions.
> Wash me thoroughly from my iniquity,
> and cleanse me from my sin.

> For I know my transgressions,
> and my sin is ever before me.
> Against you, you alone, have I sinned,
> and done what is evil in your sight,
> so that you are justified in your sentence
> and blameless when you pass judgement.
>
> You desire truth in the inward being;
> therefore teach me wisdom in my secret heart.
> Purge me with hyssop, and I shall be clean;
> wash me, and I shall be whiter than snow.
> Let me hear joy and gladness;
> Hide your face from my sins,
> and blot out all my iniquities.
>
> Create in me a clean heart, O God,
> and put a new and right spirit within me.
> Do not cast me away from your presence,
> and do not take your holy spirit from me.
> <u>Restore to me **the joy** of your salvation,</u>
> and sustain in me a willing spirit.*

There is nothing we can do for God to love us less. Too often we forget that, and our lives get off track. Joy seems to seep away from us and we find ourselves in a "far-country" without meaning and purpose.

I have been with those who were "pillars" of the church who experienced a great tragedy. They seemed to follow Kubler-Ross's stages from denial, to bargaining, to anger and get stuck there. Their anger at God is vehement. They leave the church and do not want anything to do with God. They blame God for the tragedy. They become consumed in their hate.

*Psalm 51 – selected verses

The Song Of Joy

It was in seminary that I learned that it is okay to get angry at God. I was taught as a child that one should never get angry at God or others. How thankful I was to learn that God can handle our anger. God will not break at our fist lashing out in the dark. God will not crumble at our frustrations, questions, or even our hate. Instead, God is constantly working to *"restore unto us the joy of God's salvation."*

As one who had an unusual amount of death in my life, I came to the point where I had to get in the wrestling ring with God and "slug it out". I had to know where God was in my grief, my hurt, my pain, my loss, my anger. How could I have joy in the midst of all the loss of loved ones. Was it even possible?

Even today, there are times when I receive the news that a loved one has died, I have to go back and stand in the wresting ring and face the one who can not only help me get back on the right road but receives my harsh words and blows and loves me anyway! I have experienced the "joy" of God's redeeming love even when I know I didn't deserve it.

In my first pastoral appointment a couple in the church had two young sons. The oldest 12, the youngest 9. On Christmas Eve, the nine-year-old died of leukemia. The week following Christmas, they had the service celebrating his young life and the burial.

On New Year's Eve one of the church members who had tried for several years to conceive a child, gave birth to a little girl. The next day, New Year's Day, the couple who had lost their son, went to the hospital to visit her. They bought a gift to give the new mother and father. They celebrated with them the birth of their first child even as they grieved the death of their own child.

In my years as the pastor to the couple who lost their son, I witnessed that they were still filled with joy. The parents sang in the choir, they taught in the Sunday school department, they attended the extra events of the church.

One day I said to her, "You amaze me with your faith and joy." She said, "Well, I cry just about every day in the shower, because I miss my son so badly, but nothing will keep me from serving Christ. Nothing will stop the joy I have in my heart for what Christ has done for me."

When the darkness spreads over my life, when grief and anger are acute, I remember the psalmist and I remember these who have experienced pain worse that I ever have who still have joy, and I hear God's song: I am able to restore joy to you, the kind of joy that is not fleeting, but will give you life.....life even now.....life always. God's song of joy has a melody that lets the soul smile even though we might have tears streaming down our faces and pain in our hearts.

The people who walked in darkness
have seen a great light;
those who lived in a land of deep darkness—
on them light has shined.

Isaiah 9:2 NRSV

Chapter 13

The Song of Songs

I heard about an elementary school class that was taking a test that had this question on it: "Upon what do hibernating animals subsist during the winter?" One child wrote, "All winter long hibernating animals subsist on the hope of the coming Spring." That might not have been the answer the teacher was looking for, but the child made a great point. We all subsist on the hope of the coming Spring…when new life appears.

It is a dark world without the song of resurrection.

I am reminded again and again that many of the greatest stories in the Bible happened in the dark. Creation happened in the midst of darkness and chaos, Moses lead his people out of the darkness of bondage into the wilderness toward the promised land, the birth of Jesus took place in the night as the shepherds saw the stars and followed it to find him in a manger, and Easter morning happened in the darkness of night. The followers of Jesus had put their trust in him and now he was gone. Their hopes dashed.

After the resurrection of Christ and the coming of the Holy Spirit at Pentecost, a man named Saul came into the picture. He was a devote Jew who persecuted Christians, until he had a dramatic encounter with the risen Christ and his life turned around.

He began to go everywhere he could sharing the good news of Christ's love. He became an enemy of the government and was often imprisoned and abused.

One time, he and a friend named Silas were caught and put in prison. Instead of feeling overwhelmed and fearful, they did what many would think is crazy, they sang. The prison guard came in to see what was going on and they lead him into a relationship with the risen Christ. The prison began to shake, and their chains came off. Interestingly though, they were freer in their chains than many who lived in freedom outside the jail!

When you are in the prison of grief and hopelessness, when it seems everything you try is a failure, remember to sing! Sing of God's glory, sing of God's power to transform death to life, sing of God's eternal presence with us.

Fanny Crosby was imprisoned by physical blindness all of her life, but her faith in Christ led her to see with spiritual eyes freeing her to live a long and fruitful life. She would write numerous hymns. One of my favorites went like this: "**Blessed assurance, Jesus is mine**...o what a foretaste of Glory divine. Heir of salvation, purchase of God, born of his spirit, washed in his blood. This is my story, this is my song, praising my savior all the day long!"*
Fanny Crosby had a song!

John Newton, a hated slave owner, encountered the living Christ and he left the slave trade and entered the ministry. He also had a song. He would write, **Amazing grace how sweet the sound** that saved a wretch like me, I once was lost but now am found, was blind but now I see."**

John Wesley came to America from England on a Moravian ship. When there was a huge storm at sea, he ran up the stairwell from the bottom of the ship, thinking everyone on board would be

• Crosby, Fannie. 'Blessed Assurance" Palmer's *Guide to Holiness and Revival Miscellany*, July 1873
** Newton, John. "Amazing Grace" Olney Hymns 1779

scared to death like he felt, but when he came on deck, he saw the Moravians holding onto the rails and heard them singing the songs of faith. It changed his life. He had a song, **I'll praise my maker while I've breath**. For my dad, it was **How great thou art, then sings my soul!**

What is your song of redemption, of forgiveness, of new life, of hope, of peace, of love?

Charles Wesley wrote the hymn *Christ the Lord is Risen Today*+ almost 300 years ago. He had no idea it would be sung all over the world throughout these many years. In that hymn (in verse 6) are the words *"thy power to prove"* which means that our lives bear witness to the power of the resurrection. The resurrection gives us not just a song, but a life-changing song of freedom and eternal living.

The hymn continues with the words *"thus to sing."* To be raised with Christ means to sing his song….to permit the spirit of God to sing through our lives. **Our very lives are the songs of praise to the God of love**.

The hymn: "What wondrous love is this O my soul" says,

To God and to the Lamb, I will sing, I will sing!
To God and to the Lamb, I will sing, I will sing!
To God and to the Lamb, Who is the great "I AM, "
While millions join the theme, I will sing, I will sing!
While millions join the theme, I will sing.

And when from death I'm free, I'll sing on, I'll sing on!
And when from death I'm free, I'll sing on,
And when from death I'm free, I'll sing and joyful be,
And thro' eternity, I'll sing on, I'll sing on,
And thro' eternity, I'll sing on.*

*** Wesley, John. "I'll Praise My Maker While I've Breath." 1737
+ Wesley, Charles. "Christ the Lord is Risen Today." *Hymns and Sacred Poems* hymnal. 1739
*American Folk Hymn. "What Wondrous Love Is This." UMH

I particularly love the words, "And when from death I'm free, I'll sing on I'll sing on. And through eternity, I will sing." When we are free from the death of what holds us back from following Christ, we will have the eternal song. That is, eternal life.

Wesley would also write in another hymn: "Let your ravished spirits swell, filled with endless praise and joy, in the song forever new."** When we love, love continues to grow and is ever new. So, with the love of God!

The women who went to the tomb, were in deep grief and sorrow. To their surprise the angel at the tomb of Jesus told the women to go and tell the others...he is risen...and he is going on before you. Think on these words: "going on before you."

Years ago, I was riding horses with a friend. We were going down a narrow dirt path and his horse refused to go. He tried several times, but the horse would sort of rare-up and shake himself... and turn around. So, I said, "Let me go first." My horse didn't seem to mind whatever was up ahead. We went around him and then his horse followed behind. That horse needed someone to go before him before he would trust and follow.

Sometimes in life we need someone to go ahead of us. Jesus did that for us all. He suffered and died. He knew what it was like to experience betrayal, to suffer, to feel uncomfortable and to be naked (vulnerable) in front of others. Through the power of God's great love, he overcame death, going ahead of us, and giving us new life.

Because of this, we have the greatest song in all the world. It is the song of resurrection.....of hope.....of new life....of second chances....of grace.....of forgiveness......of peace. Do you know the song that will sustain you no matter what life brings you?

** Wesley, Charles. "A Song Forever New." Hymns for Those That Seek. XXXIII 1747

The Song Of Songs

I had a woman in the church where I served as pastor who was a concert pianist. She was one of the most talented pianists I have ever heard. She held a Ph.D. in Chemistry and taught at Georgia State University. When she was 68 years old, she suffered a major stroke. It was so severe that it left her unable to move any part of her body but, her eyes, and mouth. She could not speak, but she could smile or frown. Her family put her in Christian City nursing home, and I visited her the entire 10 years I was there. But she stayed in the same room, in the same hospital bed for fourteen years before she died. Let that sink in a minute. She was in a hospital bed, day in and day out for fourteen years!

The longest I have ever stayed in a hospital bed was eight days and I thought I would climb the walls. Imagine fourteen years! Not once in those years did I ever see her frown. She would smile when I walked in and her beautiful blue eyes would light up. She would blink her eyes to answer questions I asked her: one blink for "yes" and two blinks for "no."

One of the things she loved was her tape player that was on her dresser beside the bed. She would listen for hours to beautiful music. When her husband was there, he would always play her favorite song: "The king is coming." When the song would begin, her eyes would fill with tears of joy and a huge smile would appear on her face as the words rang out:

"O the King is coming,
The King is coming!
I just heard the trumpets sounding,
And now His face I see;
O the King is coming,
The King is coming!
Praise God, He's coming for me!
Happy faces line the hallways,
Those whose lives have been redeemed,

**Broken homes that He has mended,
Those from prison He has freed;
Little children and the aged
Hand in hand stand all aglow,
<u>Who were crippled, broken, ruined,</u>**
Clad in garments white as snow.

CHORUS (repeat)

I can hear the chariots rumble,
I can see the marching throng,
The flurry of God's trumpets
Spells the end of sin and wrong:
Regal robes are now unfolding,
Heaven's grandstand's all in place,
<u>Heaven's choir now assembled,</u>
<u>Start to sing "Amazing Grace.</u>*

Though she would never play again, her song sustained her. She had a deep faith in Jesus Christ. She never lost her song. She could not sing it, but it radiated from her. She knew well the song of resurrection……the song that would sustain her day after day for 14 years.

Many people ask, "what is the proof of the resurrection: is it an empty tomb, a shroud that has the imprint of Jesus' face?" I believe the greatest proof of the resurrection of Jesus is the church. Jesus gave it to the world. It is his body. He lives and works through it… that is why it is so important. Through the church, God comes to us, individually with an eternal love, and together we are a strong force in the world for good. My parishioner that lived for 14 years in Christian City nursing home received the song from the church. It is in the church and through the church that we hear and learn the song of resurrection and eternal life.

*Milhuff,,Charles, Gloria Gaither , Willam J. Gaither.The King Is Coming lyrics © Capitol Christian Music Group

The Song Of Songs

Tony Campolo is one of the greatest preachers of our century. He is retired now as a professor at Eastman College. His home church in West Philadelphia is a 2500-member black congregation. He was the only white person in that large church.

He says he remembers when he went to his first black funeral. He was 17 years of age and a friend of his named Clarence had died. The minister was magnificent. Campolo described that preacher like this: "He preached about the resurrection and he talked about life after death in such glowing terms that I have to tell you, even at 17 I wished I was with Clarence just listening to him! He came down from the pulpit. Then he went over to the family and spoke words of comfort to them. Last of all, he went over to the open casket and for the last 20 minutes he preached to the corpse. Can you imagine that? He just yelled at the corpse. "Clarence!" "Clarence!" He spoke with great authority as he continued "Clarence you died too fast. You got away without us thanking you." He went down this litany of beautiful, wonderful things that Clarence had done for people. Then he said, "That's It, Clarence. When there's nothing more to say, there's only one thing to say, "Good night"!

"Now this is the drama," says Campolo, "White preachers can't do this, but this pastor grabbed the lid of the casket and he slammed it shut." Then he yelled "Good night Clarence!" "Good night, Clarence!"

As he slammed that lid shut he pointed to the casket and he said, "Good night Clarence, Cause I know, yes I know, that God is going to give you a good morning."

Then the choir stood up and started singing "On that great getting up morning we shall rise, we shall rise." People were upon their feet and were in the aisles hugging and kissing each other and dancing. Campolo said he was up on his feet hugging and kissing and dancing, .and he said he knew he was in the right place, because it is <u>the church</u> that can take a funeral and turn it into a celebration. *

That's what faith is all about. It's about the promise of eternal life.

Death doesn't threaten us anymore, and because of that we can sing.....really sing,....the song that **IS** eternal life."

Handel called it "Hallelujah,"
Wesley called it "Alleluia."
My grand-folks called it '"He lives".
Whatever you call it, sing it.

Sing it in the morning,
in the afternoon,
in the evening
wherever you go.

Sing it, sing it, sing it with your very life.
Sing the song that is the greatest song in the world.
Sing about the miracle of miracles!
He is risen!
He is risen and so shall we!
Hallelujah. Sing it.....Hallelujah! Yet again, sing it!
Hallelujah!
HALLELUJAH!!!!!!!
Amen.

*Campolo, Tony. Funeral Sermon. (Copied)

CPSIA information can be obtained
at www.ICGtesting.com
Printed in the USA
LVHW081615221019
634994LV00038B/2517/P